MEDITERRANEAN DIET

Cookbook

for Beginners

Easy-Made 2000 Days of Quick & Flavorful Mediterranean Recipes With No-Stress 30-Days Meal Plan | for Effortless Weight-Loss, Eating Well, Lifelong Health

Susan H. Walter

CONTENTS

Vegetable Recipes   28

Lunch & Dinner Recipes   36

Poultry Recipes   44

Other Mediterranean Recipes   83

Dessert Recipes   91

Appendix : Measurement Conversions   99

Shopping List   101

Getting to know the Mediterranean Diet

The Mediterranean diet is based on traditional foods eaten by people in countries bordering the Mediterranean Sea, including Italy, Spain, Greece, Lebanon, Cyprus, and Morocco.

Researchers have found people from these countries are generally healthier and have a lower risk for chronic diseases compared to people in many other parts of the world, and they credit this to their diets and overall lifestyle.2

The diet varies because of cultural differences, ethnic and religious backgrounds, geography, agriculture, and economy. Common factors include an emphasis on eating plenty of plant-based foods, eating dairy in moderation, and using olive oil as a primary fat source.3

Fish and poultry are more common than red meat. Wine can be consumed moderately, and fruits are a typical substitute for sugary desserts.

How to Get Started with the Mediterranean Diet

- **Focus on Whole Foods**

Highly-processed foods are not regularly consumed as part of the Mediterranean diet. If it comes in a package, check the ingredients list. When possible, try to choose foods with just whole-food ingredients like nuts, legumes or whole grains like oats and bulgur. Whole foods also include fruits, vegetables, fish and healthy plant-based oils like olive oil.

- **Make Vegetables the Main Part of Your Meal**

Fruits and vegetables should make up the bulk of your meals. The Mediterranean diet emphasizes 7 to 10 servings of fruits and vegetables each day, but even 3 to 5 servings per day have been shown to reduce the risk of cardiovascular disease. Think of small ways you can add more vegetables to your meals, like adding spinach to your eggs, loading up your sandwich with avocado and cucumber, and having an apple with nut butter, unsweetened yogurt with frozen berries, mixed nuts or oatmeal with dried fruit for a snack instead of crackers.

• Rethink Your Dairy

Instead of adding higher-saturated-fat sources of dairy like heavy cream or cheese on top of everything, aim to eat a variety of flavorful cheeses or dairy products (especially fermented dairy products) in moderation. Choose strong-flavored cheeses like feta or Parmesan where a smaller amount can satisfy the flavor you want, and try to limit intake of highly-processed cheeses, like American.

Enjoy yogurt, too, but choose plain, fermented and Greek when possible. Skip the high-added-sugar, flavored yogurts; too much added sugar can have negative health effects over time.

• Swap Red Meat for Fish

Fatty fish like salmon, mackerel, tuna and herring are the main protein sources in the Mediterranean diet. These fish contain high doses of omega-3 fatty acids, which help reduce inflammation and improve cholesterol levels. Plus, if you don't have access to fresh fish, canned versions of these fish are equally nutritious, quicker to prepare and last much longer in your pantry. White fish and shellfish are also good lean protein sources, but aren't quite as high in omega-3s. Red and highly-processed meats are eaten rarely, but rather should be enjoyed as a special occasion food. Chicken, turkey, eggs, cheese and yogurt can be enjoyed weekly or daily but in moderate portions.

• Cook with Plant-Based Oil Instead of Butter

Healthy plant-based oils like olive oil are a main fat source in the Mediterranean diet. Total fat isn't as important as the type of fat. The Mediterranean diet emphasizes eating more heart-healthy fats (poly- and monounsaturated fats) and fewer saturated and trans fats. Oils like olive oil, canola oil, avocado oil, peanut oil, sesame oil and sunflower oil are all good sources of unsaturated fat.

Saturated and trans fats can raise LDL ("bad") cholesterol if eaten in excess over time. Swap butter for heart-healthy fats like plant-based oils high in unsaturated fat to help lower your cholesterol and improve your heart health.

• Replace Refined Grains with Whole Grains

Try swapping refined grains like white bread, white rice and pasta for whole grains like corn, brown rice, quinoa, bulgur, barley and farro. Whole grains are a mainstay of the Mediterranean diet and boast a range of benefits from helping to lower cholesterol to helping stabilize blood sugars and promoting healthy weight maintenance. Whole grains are also high in B vitamins and fiber.

- **Snack on Nuts**

Don't be scared of the fat in nuts. Like plant-based oils and avocados, nuts are high in poly- and monounsaturated fats, which is the type that can benefit your heart health. They also are good sources of protein and fiber. Fat, protein and fiber are the perfect trio for staying full, keeping blood sugar stable, lowering cholesterol and reducing inflammation. To incorporate more into your day, try noshing on a quarter-cup of nuts between lunch and dinner. Walnuts have the most omega-3s, but all nuts contain healthy fats. Pair them with a fruit or vegetable if you need more to keep you full.

- **Skip the Added Sugar (Most of the Time)**

Highly-processed dessert foods like cookies, crackers, refined flours and sugars are not regularly consumed as part of the Mediterranean diet. But this doesn't mean they're totally off-limits. Instead, enjoy smaller amounts of cookies and ice cream for special occasions. Otherwise, try eat naturally-sweet foods like fruit to help satisfy sugar cravings.

- **Enjoy Red Wine in Moderation**

That's about 5 ounces (or one glass) per day for women and 10 ounces (or two glasses) per day for men. If you don't currently drink, these findings shouldn't be considered a reason to start drinking.

What are the benefits of the Mediterranean Diet?

Numerous studies have looked at the health effects of the Mediterranean diet over the years. Studies have linked the diet to lower cardiovascular risk and several other health benefits.

In one study, over a period of 12 years, women who most closely followed a Mediterranean diet had a 25% reduced risk of four cardiovascular events, including heart attack and stroke, compared to women whose diet least resembled a Mediterranean diet.

Among the health benefits of following a Mediterranean diet is lower risk of the following:

- cardiovascular disease

- heart attack

- stroke

- various types of cancer

- Parkinson's disease

- Alzheimer's disease

- type 2 diabetes

- rheumatoid arthritis

- nonalcoholic fatty liver.

MEDITERRANEAN DIET

Researchers have also studied associations between a Mediterranean diet and aging. One study of over 10,000 women ages 57 to 61 found that women who followed a Mediterranean-type eating pattern were 46% more likely to live to 70 or older without chronic disease.

The health benefits of this eating style make it a top recommendation for health experts. The American Heart Association (AHA) recommends the diet for the role it can play in preventing heart disease and stroke, and reducing risk factors such as obesity, diabetes, high cholesterol, and high blood pressure. In addition, the USDA's Dietary Guidelines for Americans, 2020–2025 supports a healthy Mediterranean-style pattern.

Reasons for recommending a Mediterranean cookbook

Health Benefits: The Mediterranean diet is known for its health benefits, including lower rates of heart disease, diabetes, and obesity. A Mediterranean cookbook can help you incorporate these healthy eating habits into your daily life.

Delicious and Flavorful: Mediterranean cuisine is famous for its delicious and flavorful dishes. From Greek souvlaki to Italian pasta dishes and Spanish paella, there is a wide variety of mouthwatering recipes to explore.

Diverse Ingredients: Mediterranean cuisine features a wide range of ingredients, including fresh fruits and vegetables, olive oil, whole grains, lean proteins, and aromatic herbs and spices. Learning to cook with these ingredients can introduce you to new flavors and cooking techniques.

Cultural Exploration: Cooking Mediterranean recipes allows you to explore the diverse cultures and traditions of the Mediterranean region. You can learn about the culinary heritage of countries like Greece, Italy, Spain, Morocco, and more.

Versatility: Mediterranean cuisine is versatile and can accommodate various dietary preferences and restrictions. Whether you're a meat lover, vegetarian, or follow a specific dietary plan, you can find Mediterranean recipes that suit your needs.

Easy and Accessible: Many Mediterranean recipes are simple to prepare and use readily available ingredients. This makes it easy for both beginners and experienced cooks to enjoy Mediterranean dishes at home.

DAY	BREAKFAST	LUNCH	DINNER
1	Mediterranean Frittata 15	Hoemade Egg Drop Soup 29	Minted Roasted Leg Of Lamb 37
2	Farro Salad 15	Mediterranean Diet Styled Stuffed Peppers 29	Ground Pork And Tomatoes Soup 37
3	Mushroom Bake 15	Collard Green Wrap Greek Style 29	Quinoa Zucchini Stew 37
4	Thyme Breakfast Pizza (zaatar Manakish) 15	Parsnips With Eggplant 30	Quinoa Chicken Casserole 37
5	Avocado Toast 16	Feta And Roasted Eggplant Dip 30	Summer Fish Stew 38
6	Parmesan Cauliflower Cakes 16	Cardamom And Carrot Soup 30	Pistachio Crusted Lamb Chops 38
7	Bulgur Bowls 16	Basil Corn 30	Moroccan spices Crusted Sea Bass 38
8	Blueberries Quinoa 16	Sage Artichokes 31	Chicken Zucchini Ragout 39
9	Sage Omelet 17	Zucchini Tomato Potato Ratatouille 31	Olive Oil Lemon Broiled Cod 39
10	Bacon, Spinach And Tomato Sandwich 17	Mediterranean Grilled Cheese Sandwiches 31	Veggie Soup 39
11	Spinach Pie 17	Vegetarian Stuffed Baked Potatoes 32	Lamb Soup 40
12	Bacon, Vegetable And Parmesan Combo 18	Thyme Mushrooms 32	Roasted Vegetables And Chorizo 40
13	Fruits And Pistachios 17	Provolone Over Herbed Portobello Mushrooms 32	Spice-rubbed Beef Steaks 40
14	Cream Olive Muffins 18	Soy Eggplants 33	Buttermilk Marinated Roast Chicken 41
15	Cheesy Eggs Ramekins 18	Instant Pot Artichoke Hearts 33	Pork And Prunes Stew 41

DAY	BREAKFAST	LUNCH	DINNER
16	Garlic Scrambled Eggs 18	Coconut Squash Flowers 33	Creamy Chicken Soup 42
17	Mediterranean Omelet 18	Vegetarian Potato Kibbeh 34	Tomato Roasted Feta 42
18	Pesto Portobello Omelet 19	Avocado Salad 34	Sausage Ragout 42
19	Banana Quinoa 19	Almond Kale 35	Mediterranean Tarts 43
20	Potato Cakes 19	Spicy Potato Salad 41	Greek Beef Meatballs 43
21	Eggs With Zucchini Noodles 20	Tuna And Spinach Salad 41	Chicken And Ginger Cucumbers Mix 45
22	Cheesy Olives Bread 20	Chorizo-kidney Beans Quinoa Pilaf 60	Herbed Almond Turkey 45
23	Milk Scones 20	Pesto Chicken Pasta 60	Ginger Chicken Drumsticks 45
24	Collard Green Chicken Roll Ups 23	Mediterranean Diet Pasta With Mussels 61	Chicken And Lemongrass Sauce 45
25	Cucumber Rolls 24	Tortellini Salad With Broccoli 60	Creamy Chicken 46
26	Chickpeas And Eggplant Bowls 26	Blue Cheese And Grains Salad 61	Chicken With Artichokes And Beans 46
27	Spinach Pies 17	Chickpea-crouton Kale Caesar Salad 62	Parmesan Chicken And Pineapple 46
28	Cucumber Bites 27	Tasty Lasagna Rolls 62	Chicken And Tzaziki Pitas 46
29	Mediterranean Frittata 15	Sun-dried Tomatoes And Chickpeas 62	Chicken With Spinach 47
30	Farro Salad 15	Kefta Styled Beef Patties With Cucumber Salad 63	Lemon Chicken Mix 47

Breakfast Recipes

Breakfast Recipes

Mediterranean Frittata

Servings: 6
Cooking Time:15 Minutes

Ingredients:
- 8 eggs
- 3 tablespoons olive oil, divided
- 2 tablespoons Parmesan cheese, finely shredded
- 1/8 teaspoon ground black pepper
- 1/4 cup low-fat milk
- 1/4 cup fresh basil, slivered
- 1/2 of a 7-ounce jar (about 1/2 cup) roasted red sweet peppers, drained, chopped
- 1/2 cup onion-and-garlic croutons, purchased, coarsely crushed
- 1/2 cup kalamata or ripe olives, sliced, pitted
- 1/2 cup (2 ounces) feta cheese, crumbled
- 1 teaspoon garlic, bottled minced
- 1 cup onion, chopped

Directions:
1. Preheat broiler.
2. In a cast-iron skillet over medium heat, heat 2 table-spoons of the olive oil. Add the garlic and the onion; cook until the onions are just tender.
3. In a large bowl, combine the eggs and the milk; beat. Stir in the feta, sweet peppers, basil, olives, and black pepper. Pour the egg mixture into the skillet and cook. As the mixture sets, using a spatula, lift the egg mixture to allow the uncooked liquid to flow underneath. Continue cooking and lifting until the egg is almost set but the surface is still moist. Reduce the heat, if necessary, to prevent overcooking.
4. In a small-sized bowl, combine the parmesan, croutons, and the remaining 1 tablespoon of olive oil; sprinkle the mixture over the frittata.
5. Transfer the skillet under the broiler about 4-5 inches from the source of heat; broil for about 1-2 minutes, or until the top is set.

Nutrition Info:
- Per Serving:242 Cal, 19 g total fat (6 g sat. fat), 297 mg chol., 339 mg sodium, 7g carb.,1 g fiber,12 g protein.

Farro Salad

Servings: 2
Cooking Time: 4 Minutes

Ingredients:
- 1 tablespoon olive oil
- A pinch of salt and black pepper
- 1 bunch baby spinach, chopped
- 1 avocado, pitted, peeled and chopped
- 1 garlic clove, minced
- 2 cups farro, already cooked
- ½ cup cherry tomatoes, cubed

Directions:
1. Heat up a pan with the oil over medium heat, add the spinach, and the rest of the ingredients, toss, cook for 4 minutes, divide into bowls and serve.

Nutrition Info:
- calories 157, fat 13.7, fiber 5.5, carbs 8.6, protein 3.6

Mushroom Bake

Servings: 3
Cooking Time: 25 Minutes

Ingredients:
- ½ cup mushrooms, chopped
- ½ yellow onion, diced
- 4 eggs, beaten
- 1 tablespoon coconut flakes
- ½ teaspoon chili pepper
- 1 oz Cheddar cheese, shredded
- 1 teaspoon canola oil

Directions:
1. Pour canola oil in the skillet and preheat well.
2. Add mushrooms and onion and roast for 5-8 minutes or until the vegetables are light brown.
3. Transfer the cooked vegetables in the casserole mold.
4. Add coconut flakes, chili pepper, and Cheddar cheese.
5. Then add eggs and stir well.
6. Bake the casserole for 15 minutes at 360F.

Nutrition Info:
- Per Servingcalories 152, fat 11.1, fiber 0.7, carbs 3, protein 10.4

Thyme Breakfast Pizza (zaatar Manakish)

Serves: 1 Pizza
Cooking Time:10 Minutes

Ingredients:
- 1 cup zaatar
- 1/2 cup extra-virgin olive oil
- 1 batch Multipurpose Dough (recipe in Chapter 12)
- 1/4 cup all-purpose flour

Directions:
1. Preheat the oven to 400ºF. Flour a rolling pin and your

counter.

2. Divide Multipurpose Dough into 6 equal portions, and roll out dough into 6- to 8-inch-diameter circles.

3. In a small bowl, combine zaatar with extra-virgin olive oil. Spread 2 or 3 tablespoons zaatar mixture onto each dough circle.

4. Place pizzas onto a baking sheet, and bake for 8 to 10 minutes or until zaatar begins to bubble.

5. Remove pizzas from the oven, fold each pizza in half, enjoy as is or with Yogurt Spread (Labne; recipe in Chapter 3).

Avocado Toast

Servings: 2
Cooking Time: 0 Minutes

Ingredients:

- 1 tablespoon goat cheese, crumbled
- 1 avocado, peeled, pitted and mashed
- A pinch of salt and black pepper
- 2 whole wheat bread slices, toasted
- ½ teaspoon lime juice
- 1 persimmon, thinly sliced
- 1 fennel bulb, thinly sliced
- 2 teaspoons honey
- 2 tablespoons pomegranate seeds

Directions:

1. In a bowl, combine the avocado flesh with salt, pepper, lime juice and the cheese and whisk.

2. Spread this onto toasted bread slices, top each slice with the remaining ingredients and serve for breakfast.

Nutrition Info:

- calories 348, fat 20.8, fiber 12.3, carbs 38.7, protein 7.1

Parmesan Cauliflower Cakes

Servings: 2
Cooking Time: 10 Minutes

Ingredients:

- 1 cup cauliflower, shredded
- 1 egg, beaten
- 1 tablespoon wheat flour, whole grain
- 1 oz Parmesan, grated
- ½ teaspoon ground black pepper
- 1 tablespoon canola oil

Directions:

1. In the mixing bowl mix up together shredded cauliflower and egg.

2. Add wheat flour, grated Parmesan, and ground black pepper.

3. Stir the mixture with the help of the fork until it is homogenous and smooth.

4. Pour canola oil in the skillet and bring it to boil.

5. Make the fritters from the cauliflower mixture with the help of the fingertips or use spoon and transfer in the hot oil.

6. Roast the fritters for 4 minutes from each side over the medium-low heat.

Nutrition Info:

- Per Servingcalories 167, fat 12.3, fiber 1.5, carbs 6.7, protein 8.8

Bulgur Bowls

Servings: 3
Cooking Time: 15 Minutes

Ingredients:

- 1 cup bulgur
- 2 cups Greek yogurt
- 1 ½ cup water
- ½ teaspoon salt
- 1 teaspoon olive oil

Directions:

1. Pour olive oil in the saucepan and add bulgur.

2. Roast it over the medium heat for 2-3 minutes. Stir it from time to time.

3. After this, add salt and water.

4. Close the lid and cook bulgur for 15 minutes over the medium heat.

5. Then chill the cooked bulgur well and combine it with Greek yogurt. Stir it carefully.

6. Transfer the cooked meal into the serving plates. The yogurt bulgur tastes the best when it is cold.

Nutrition Info:

- Per Servingcalories 274, fat 4.9, fiber 8.5, carbs 40.8, protein 19.2

Blueberries Quinoa

Servings: 4
Cooking Time: 0 Minutes

Ingredients:

- 2 cups almond milk
- 2 cups quinoa, already cooked
- ½ teaspoon cinnamon powder
- 1 tablespoon honey
- 1 cup blueberries
- ¼ cup walnuts, chopped

Directions:

1. In a bowl, mix the quinoa with the milk and the rest of the ingredients, toss, divide into smaller bowls and serve for breakfast.

Nutrition Info:

- calories 284, fat 14.3, fiber 3.2, carbs 15.4, protein 4.4

Sage Omelet

Servings: 8
Cooking Time: 25 Minutes

Ingredients:
- 8 eggs, beaten
- 6 oz Goat cheese, crumbled
- ½ teaspoon salt
- 3 tablespoons sour cream
- 1 teaspoon butter
- ½ teaspoon canola oil
- ¼ teaspoon sage
- ¼ teaspoon dried oregano
- 1 teaspoon chives, chopped

Directions:
1. Put butter in the skillet. Add canola oil and preheat the mixture until it is homogenous.
2. Meanwhile, in the mixing bowl combine together salt, sour cream, sage, dried oregano, and chives. Add eggs and stir the mixture carefully with the help of the spoon/fork.
3. Pour the egg mixture in the skillet with butter-oil liquid.
4. Sprinkle the omelet with goat cheese and close the lid.
5. Cook the breakfast for 20 minutes over the low heat. The cooked omelet should be solid.
6. Slice it into the servings and transfer in the plates.

Nutrition Info:
- Per Servingcalories 176, fat 13.7, fiber 0, carbs 0, protein 12.2

Bacon, Spinach And Tomato Sandwich

Servings: 1
Cooking Time: 0 Minutes

Ingredients:
- 2 whole-wheat bread slices, toasted
- 1 tablespoon Dijon mustard
- 3 bacon slices
- Salt and black pepper to the taste
- 2 tomato slices
- ¼ cup baby spinach

Directions:
1. Spread the mustard on each bread slice, divide the bacon and the rest of the ingredients on one slice, top with the other one, cut in half and serve for breakfast.

Nutrition Info:
- calories 246, fat 11.2, fiber 4.5, carbs 17.5, protein 8.3

Spinach Pie

Servings: 6
Cooking Time: 1 Hour

Ingredients:
- 2 cups spinach
- 1 white onion, diced

- ½ cup fresh parsley
- 1 teaspoon minced garlic
- 3 oz Feta cheese, crumbled
- 1 teaspoon ground paprika
- 2 eggs, beaten
- 1/3 cup butter, melted
- 2 oz Phyllo dough

Directions:
1. Separate Phyllo dough into 2 parts.
2. Brush the casserole mold with butter well and place 1 part of Phyllo dough inside.
3. Brush its surface with butter too.
4. Put the spinach and fresh parsley in the blender. Blend it until smooth and transfer in the mixing bowl.
5. Add minced garlic, Feta cheese, ground paprika, eggs, and diced onion. Mix up well.
6. Place the spinach mixture in the casserole mold and flatten it well.
7. Cover the spinach mixture with remaining Phyllo dough and pour remaining butter over it.
8. Bake spanakopita for 1 hour at 350F.
9. Cut it into the servings.

Nutrition Info:
- Per Servingcalories 190, fat 15.4, fiber 1.1, carbs 8.4, protein 5.4

Fruits And Pistachios

Servings: 12
Cooking Time:7 Minutes

Ingredients:
- 1 1/2 cups pistachios, unsalted, roasted
- 1/2 cup dried apricots, chopped (preferably Blenheim)
- 1/2 teaspoon cinnamon
- 1/4 cup dried cranberries or pomegranate seeds
- 1/4 teaspoon nutmeg, regular ground or freshly grated
- 1/4 teaspoon ground allspice
- 2 teaspoons sugar

Directions:
1. Preheat oven to 350F.
2. Spread the pistachios into a rimmed baking sheet; bake for about 7 minutes or until lightly toasted. Cool completely.
3. In a bowl, toss the pistachios with the apricots, pomegranate seeds, cinnamon, nutmeg, allspice, and sugar until well coated.

Nutrition Info:
- Per Serving:116 Cal, 7.1 g total fat (0.9 g sat. fat), 0.0 mg chol., 2.4 mg sodium, 11 g carb.,2.1 g fiber, 3.5 g protein.

Bacon, Vegetable And Parmesan Combo

Servings: 2
Cooking Time: 25 Minutes

Ingredients:
- 2 slices of bacon, thick-cut
- ½ tbsp mayonnaise
- ½ of medium green bell pepper, deseeded, chopped
- 1 scallion, chopped
- ¼ cup grated Parmesan cheese
- 1 tbsp olive oil

Directions:
1. Switch on the oven, then set its temperature to 375°F and let it preheat.
2. Meanwhile, take a baking dish, grease it with oil, and add slices of bacon in it.
3. Spread mayonnaise on top of the bacon, then top with bell peppers and scallions, sprinkle with Parmesan cheese and bake for about 25 minutes until cooked thoroughly.
4. When done, take out the baking dish and serve immediately.
5. For meal prepping, wrap bacon in a plastic sheet and refrigerate for up to 2 days.
6. When ready to eat, reheat bacon in the microwave and then serve.

Nutrition Info:
- Calories 197, Total Fat 13.8g, Total Carbs 4.7g, Protein 14.3g, Sugar 1.9g, Sodium 662mg

Cream Olive Muffins

Servings: 6
Cooking Time: 20 Minutes

Ingredients:
- ½ cup quinoa, cooked
- 2 oz Feta cheese, crumbled
- 2 eggs, beaten
- 3 kalamata olives, chopped
- ¾ cup heavy cream
- 1 tomato, chopped
- 1 teaspoon butter, softened
- 1 tablespoon wheat flour, whole grain
- ½ teaspoon salt

Directions:
1. In the mixing bowl whisk eggs and add Feta cheese.
2. Then add chopped tomato and heavy cream.
3. After this, add wheat flour, salt, and quinoa.
4. Then add kalamata olives and mix up the ingredients with the help of the spoon.
5. Brush the muffin molds with the butter from inside.
6. Transfer quinoa mixture in the muffin molds and flatten it with the help of the spatula or spoon if needed.
7. Cook the muffins in the preheated to 355F oven for 20

minutes.

Nutrition Info:
- Per Servingcalories 165, fat 10.8, fiber 1.2, carbs 11.5, protein 5.8

Cheesy Eggs Ramekins

Servings: 2
Cooking Time: 10 Minutes

Ingredients:
- 1 tablespoon chives, chopped
- 1 tablespoon dill, chopped
- A pinch of salt and black pepper
- 2 tablespoons cheddar cheese, grated
- 1 tomato, chopped
- 2 eggs, whisked
- Cooking spray

Directions:
1. In a bowl, mix the eggs with the tomato and the rest of the ingredients except the cooking spray and whisk well.
2. Grease 2 ramekins with the cooking spray, divide the mix into each ramekin, bake at 400 degrees F for 10 minutes and serve.

Nutrition Info:
- calories 104, fat 7.1, fiber 0.6, carbs 2.6, protein 7.9

Garlic Scrambled Eggs

Serves:½ Cup
Cooking Time:10 Minutes

Ingredients:
- 1/4 lb. ground beef
- 2 TB. extra-virgin olive oil
- 1/2 tsp. salt
- 1 TB. garlic, finely chopped
- 4 large eggs
- 1/2 tsp. ground black pepper

Directions:
1. In a nonstick pan over medium heat, brown beef for 5 minutes, breaking up chunks with a wooden spoon.
2. Add extra-virgin olive oil, salt, and garlic, cook for 3 more minutes.
3. Break eggs into the pan, stir eggs into beef and garlic mixture, and cook for 2 more minutes.
4. Season with black pepper, and serve warm.

Mediterranean Omelet

Serves:1 Omelet
Cooking Time:10 Minutes

Ingredients:
- 2 TB. extra-virgin olive oil
- 2 TB. yellow onion, finely chopped
- 1 small clove garlic, minced

- 1/2 tsp. salt
- 1 cup fresh spinach, chopped
- 1/2 medium tomato, diced
- 2 large eggs
- 2 TB. whole or 2 percent milk
- 4 kalamata olives, pitted and chopped
- 1/2 tsp. ground black pepper
- 3 TB. crumbled feta cheese
- 1 TB. fresh parsley, finely chopped

Directions:

1. In a nonstick pan over medium heat, cook extra-virgin olive oil, yellow onion, and garlic for 3 minutes.
2. Add salt, spinach, and tomato, and cook for 4 minutes.
3. In a small bowl, whisk together eggs and whole milk.
4. Add kalamata olives and black pepper to the pan, and pour in eggs over sautéed vegetables.
5. Using a rubber spatula, slowly push down edges of eggs, letting raw egg form a new layer, and continue for about 2 minutes or until eggs are cooked.
6. Fold omelet in half, and slide onto a plate. Top with feta cheese and fresh parsley, and serve warm.

Pesto Portobello Omelet

Servings:1
Cooking Time:15 Minutes

Ingredients:
- 4 egg whites (or 3 eggs)
- 1 Portobello mushroom cap, sliced
- 1/4 cup mozzarella cheese, low-fat, shredded
- 1/4 cup red onion, chopped
- 1 teaspoon prepared pesto
- 1 teaspoon olive oil
- 1 teaspoon water
- Salt and ground black pepper, to taste

Directions:

1. In a skillet, heat the olive oil over medium heat. Add the mushrooms and the onion; cook for about 3-5 minutes until the mushrooms are soft.
2. In a small bowl, whisk the water and the egg whites together and pour over the mushrooms and onions in the skillet. Season with salt and pepper; cook for about 5 minutes, occasionally stirring, until the egg whites are no longer runny.
3. Sprinkle mozzarella over and top with pesto. Fold the omelet in half; continue cooking for about 2-3 minutes or until the cheese melts.

Nutrition Info:
- Per Serving:241 Cal, 12.3 g total fat (4.1 g sat. fat), 16 mg chol., 341 mg sodium, 7.9 g carb., 1.6 g fiber, 25.9 g protein.

Banana Quinoa

Servings: 4
Cooking Time: 12 Minutes

Ingredients:
- 1 cup quinoa
- 2 cup milk
- 1 teaspoon vanilla extract
- 1 teaspoon honey
- 2 bananas, sliced
- ¼ teaspoon ground cinnamon

Directions:

1. Pour milk in the saucepan and add quinoa.
2. Close the lid and cook it over the medium heat for 12 minutes or until quinoa will absorb all liquid.
3. Then chill the quinoa for 10-15 minutes and place in the serving mason jars.
4. Add honey, vanilla extract, and ground cinnamon.
5. Stir well.
6. Top quinoa with banana and stir it before serving.

Nutrition Info:
- Calories 279, fat 5.3, fiber 4.6, carbs 48.4, protein 10.7

Potato Cakes

Servings: 4
Cooking Time: 6 Minutes

Ingredients:
- 2 potatoes, peeled
- ½ onion, diced
- ½ cup spinach, chopped
- 2 eggs, beaten
- ½ teaspoon salt
- ½ teaspoon ground black pepper
- 1 teaspoon olive oil

Directions:

1. Grate the potato and mix it with chopped spinach, diced onion, salt, and ground black pepper.
2. Add eggs and stir until homogenous.
3. Then pour olive oil in the skillet and preheat it well.
4. Make the medium latkes with the help of 2 spoons and transfer them in the preheated oil.
5. Roast the latkes for 3 minutes from each side or until they are golden brown.
6. Dry the cooked latkes with the help of the paper towel if needed.

Nutrition Info:
- Per Servingcalories 122, fat 3.5, fiber 3, carbs 18.5, protein 4.9

Eggs With Zucchini Noodles

Servings: 2
Cooking Time: 11 Minutes

Ingredients:

- 2 tablespoons extra-virgin olive oil
- 3 zucchinis, cut with a spiralizer
- 4 eggs
- Salt and black pepper to the taste
- A pinch of red pepper flakes
- Cooking spray
- 1 tablespoon basil, chopped

Directions:

1. In a bowl, combine the zucchini noodles with salt, pepper and the olive oil and toss well.
2. Grease a baking sheet with cooking spray and divide the zucchini noodles into 4 nests on it.
3. Crack an egg on top of each nest, sprinkle salt, pepper and the pepper flakes on top and bake at 350 degrees F for 11 minutes.
4. Divide the mix between plates, sprinkle the basil on top and serve.

Nutrition Info:

- calories 296, fat 23.6, fiber 3.3, carbs 10.6, protein 14.7

Cheesy Olives Bread

Servings: 10
Cooking Time: 30 Minutes

Ingredients:

- 4 cups whole-wheat flour
- 3 tablespoons oregano, chopped
- 2 teaspoons dry yeast
- ¼ cup olive oil
- 1 and ½ cups black olives, pitted and sliced
- 1 cup water
- ½ cup feta cheese, crumbled

Directions:

1. In a bowl, mix the flour with the water, the yeast and the oil, stir and knead your dough very well.
2. Put the dough in a bowl, cover with plastic wrap and keep in a warm place for 1 hour.
3. Divide the dough into 2 bowls and stretch each ball really well.
4. Add the rest of the ingredients on each ball and tuck them inside well kneading the dough again.
5. Flatten the balls a bit and leave them aside for 40 minutes more.
6. Transfer the balls to a baking sheet lined with parchment paper, make a small slit in each and bake at 425 degrees F for 30 minutes.
7. Serve the bread as a Mediterranean breakfast.

Nutrition Info:

- calories 251, fat 7.3, fiber 2.1, carbs 39.7, protein 6.7

Milk Scones

Servings: 4
Cooking Time: 10 Minutes

Ingredients:

- ½ cup wheat flour, whole grain
- 1 teaspoon baking powder
- 1 tablespoon butter, melted
- 1 teaspoon vanilla extract
- 1 egg, beaten
- ¾ teaspoon salt
- 3 tablespoons milk
- 1 teaspoon vanilla sugar

Directions:

1. In the mixing bowl combine together wheat flour, baking powder, butter, vanilla extract, and egg. Add salt and knead the soft and non-sticky dough. Add more flour if needed.
2. Then make the log from the dough and cut it into the triangles.
3. Line the tray with baking paper.
4. Arrange the dough triangles on the baking paper and transfer in the preheat to the 360F oven.
5. Cook the scones for 10 minutes or until they are light brown.
6. After this, chill the scones and brush with milk and sprinkle with vanilla sugar.

Nutrition Info:

• Per Servingcalories 112, fat 4.4, fiber 0.5, carbs 14.3, protein 3.4

Snack And Appetizer Recipes

Snack And Appetizer Recipes

Cucumber Roll Ups

Servings: 6
Cooking Time: 15 Minutes

Ingredients:
- 1 large cucumber
- 1/8 teaspoon ground black pepper
- 6 tablespoons feta, crumbled
- 6 tablespoons roasted garlic hummus
- 6 tablespoons roasted red pepper, chopped

Directions:
1. With a vegetable peeler, shave off long thin cucumber slices. Alternatively, you can use a sharp knife to cut the cucumber into thin slices. Do not use the inner part of the cucumber that is full of seeds. You should be able to get 12 slices.
2. Sprinkle each slice with a pinch of black pepper. Evenly spread about 1 1/2 teaspoon of hummus on each slice. Sprinkle with the red pepper and with 1 1/2 teaspoon of feta over each slice.
3. Pick one end and roll each cucumber around the filling, making sure not to roll them too tightly or the filling will squeeze out. With the seam on the bottom, place each rolling a serving plate. Secure each piece by sticking a toothpick through the center of each roll.

Nutrition Info:
- Per Serving:64 cal, 5 g total fat (1.9 sat. fat), 3.4 g carbs, 0.7 g fiber, and 2.5 g protein.

Goat Cheese And Chives Spread

Servings: 4
Cooking Time: 0 Minutes

Ingredients:
- 2 ounces goat cheese, crumbled
- ¾ cup sour cream
- 2 tablespoons chives, chopped
- 1 tablespoon lemon juice
- Salt and black pepper to the taste
- 2 tablespoons extra virgin olive oil

Directions:
1. In a bowl, mix the goat cheese with the cream and the rest of the ingredients and whisk really well.
2. Keep in the fridge for 10 minutes and serve as a party spread.

Nutrition Info:
- calories 220, fat 11.5, fiber 4.8, carbs 8.9, protein 5.6

Eggplant Bombs

Servings: 6
Cooking Time: 45 Minutes

Ingredients:
- 4 cups eggplants, chopped
- 3 tablespoons olive oil
- 3 garlic cloves, minced
- 2 eggs, whisked
- Salt and black pepper to the taste
- 1 cup parsley, chopped
- ½ cup parmesan cheese, finely grated
- ¾ cups bread crumbs

Directions:
1. Heat up a pan with the oil over medium high heat, add the garlic and the eggplants, and cook for 15 minutes stirring often.
2. In a bowl, combine the eggplant mix with the rest of the ingredients, stir well and shape medium balls out of this mix.
3. Arrange the balls on a baking sheet lined with parchment paper and bake at 350 degrees F for 30 minutes.
4. Serve as a snack.

Nutrition Info:
- calories 224, fat 10.6, fiber 1.8, carbs 5.4, protein 3.5

Turmeric Cauliflower Bites

Servings:6
Cooking Time: 12 Minutes

Ingredients:
- 1-pound cauliflower head, trimmed
- 3 tablespoons lemon juice
- 3 eggs, beaten
- 1 teaspoon salt
- 1 teaspoon ground black pepper
- 2 cups water, for cooking
- 3 tablespoons almond butter
- 1 teaspoon turmeric

Directions:
1. Place the cauliflower head in the pan.
2. Add water.
3. Boil the cauliflower for 8 minutes or until it is tender.
4. Then cool the vegetable well and separate it onto the florets.
5. Whisk together beaten eggs, salt, ground black pepper, and turmeric.
6. Dip every cauliflower floret in the egg mixture.
7. Toss the almond butter in the skillet and heat it up.

8. Roast the cauliflower florets for 2 minutes from each side over the medium heat.

9. When the cauliflower florets are golden brown, they are cooked.

10. Sprinkle the cooked florets with lemon juice.

Nutrition Info:

• Per Servingcalories 103, fat 6.9, fiber 2.9, carbs 6.3, protein 6.1

Tomato Bites

Servings:4
Cooking Time: 5 Minutes

Ingredients:

• 6 oz chorizo, sliced
• 1 teaspoon tomato paste
• 1 tablespoon almond butter
• 1 teaspoon cayenne pepper
• ½ teaspoon honey
• 3 tablespoons water

Directions:

1. Melt almond butter in the skillet.
2. Place sliced chorizo and sprinkle it with cayenne pepper.
3. Roast chorizo for 2 minutes from each side.
4. Meanwhile, mix up together water, honey, and tomato paste.
5. Add the mixture in chorizo and stir well.
6. Cook the meal for 1 minute more.
7. Pin every chorizo slice with a toothpick for more comfortable eating.

Nutrition Info:

• Per Servingcalories 223, fat 18.6, fiber 0.6, carbs 2.8, protein 11.2

Flavorful Roasted Baby Potatoes

Servings: 4
Cooking Time: 10 Minutes

Ingredients:

• 2 lbs baby potatoes, clean and cut in half
• 1/2 cup vegetable stock
• 1 tsp paprika
• 3/4 tsp garlic powder
• 1 tsp onion powder
• 2 tsp Italian seasoning
• 1 tbsp olive oil
• Pepper
• Salt

Directions:

1. Add oil into the inner pot of instant pot and set the pot on sauté mode.
2. Add potatoes and sauté for 5 minutes. Add remaining ingredients and stir well.

3. Seal pot with lid and cook on high for 5 minutes.
4. Once done, release pressure using quick release. Remove lid.
5. Stir well and serve.

Nutrition Info:

• Calories 175 Fat 4.5 g Carbohydrates 29.8 g Sugar 0.7 g Protein 6.1 g Cholesterol 2 mg

Collard Green Chicken Roll Ups

Servings: 4
Cooking Time:20 Minutes

Ingredients:

• 4 large collard greens
• 1/2 teaspoon hot sauce
• 1/2 cup black olives, diced
• 1 tablespoon fresh cilantro, de-stemmed and chopped
• 1 small seedless cucumber cut into long match sticks
• 1 pound of Foster Farms Simply Raised chicken
• 1 large avocado
• Juice of 1/2 lime
• Salt and pepper, to taste

Directions:

1. Place a large-sized grill pan over medium heat. Season both sides of the chicken with the salt and pepper. Place on the grill, cook until the meat is no longer pink and opaque all the way through. Remove from the heat.

2. Meanwhile, fill the bottom of a large skillet with few inches of water; bring to a boil over high heat. Ready a large-sized bowl filled with iced cubes and cold water near the stove.

3. Slice off the stems and the tough backbones from the collard greens using a paring knife.

4. Add one leaf at a time into the boiling water, blanching for about 30 to 45 seconds until they are pliable but not soft to fall apart when rolled. Remove from the boiling water and immediately add to the iced water, letting the water cool. Once cool, place the leaf on a paper towel or dish towel; dry well. Repeat the process with the remaining leaves.

5. Place the avocado in a bowl, add the cilantro, lime, hot sauce, and season with salt and pepper to taste; mash together to combine.

6. Place a leaf on a clean, flat surface. Spread a dollop of the avocado mixture at the larger part of the collard greens. Top the avocado mixture with the chicken, cucumber, and olives.

7. Fold the top end of the collard over the filling; roll the leaf, tucking in the sides as you roll the bottom. Cut the rolls into halves; serve.

Nutrition Info:

• Per Serving:250 cal., 13 g total fat (2.5 g sat. fat), 75 mg chol., 450 mg sodium, 670 mg pot., 12 g total carbs., 6 g fiber, 2 g sugar, 25 g protein, 4% vitamin A, 20% vitamin C, 6% calcium, and15% iron.

Cauliflower Spread

Servings:4
Cooking Time: 15 Minutes

Ingredients:
- 1 cup cauliflower
- 1 teaspoon tahini paste
- 3 tablespoons lemon juice
- ½ teaspoon minced garlic
- 1 teaspoon dried oregano
- ¼ teaspoon cayenne pepper
- ½ teaspoon salt
- ¼ teaspoon dried thyme
- 1 cup of water

Directions:
1. Pour water in the pan and add cauliflower.
2. Boil cauliflower for 15 minutes.
3. Then drain ½ part of liquid from cauliflower.
4. Transfer remaining liquid and cauliflower in the food processor.
5. Add tahini paste, lemon juice, minced garlic, dried oregano, cayenne pepper, salt, and dried thyme.
6. Blend the mixture until you get a smooth and fluffy mixture.
7. Store the cooked hummus in the fridge up to 3 days.

Nutrition Info:
- Per Servingcalories 19, fat 0.9, fiber 1, carbs 2.3, protein 0.9

Mozzarella Chips

Servings:8
Cooking Time: 10 Minutes

Ingredients:
- 4 phyllo dough sheets
- 4 oz Mozzarella, shredded
- 1 tablespoon olive oil

Directions:
1. Place 2 phyllo sheets in the pan and brush it with sprinkle it with Mozzarella.
2. Then cover the cheese with 2 remaining phyllo sheets.
3. Brush the top of Phyllo with olive oil and cut on 8 squares.
4. Bake the chips for 10 minutes at 365F or until they are light brown.

Nutrition Info:
- Per Servingcalories 130, fat 5, fiber 0.5, carbs 15.5, protein 6.5

Calamari Mediterranean

Servings:2
Cooking Time:10 Minutes

Ingredients:
- 1 tablespoon Italian parsley
- 1 teaspoon ancho chili, chopped
- 1 teaspoon cumin
- 1 teaspoon red pepper flakes
- 1/2 cup white wine
- 2 cups calamari
- 2 medium plum tomatoes, diced
- 2 tablespoons capers
- 2 tablespoons garlic cloves, roasted
- 2 tablespoons olive oil
- 2 tablespoons unsalted butter
- 3 tablespoons lime juice
- Salt

Directions:
1. Heat a sauté pan. Add the oil, garlic, and the calamari; sauté for 1 minute. Add the capers, red pepper flakes, cumin, ancho chili and the diced tomatoes; cook for 1 minute.
2. Add the wine and the lime juice; simmer for 4 minutes.
3. Stir in the butter, parsley, and the salt; continue cooking until the sauce is thick.
4. Serve with whole-wheat French bread.

Nutrition Info:
- Per Serving:308.8 cal., 25.7 g total fat (9.3 sat. fat), 30.5 mg chol., 267.8 mg sodium, 10.2 g total carbs., 1.7 g fiber, 2.8 g sugar, and 1.9 g protein.

Feta Cheese Log With Sun-dried Tomatoes And Kalamata Olives

Servings:2
Cooking Time: 20 Minutes

Ingredients:
- 8 ounces feta cheese, crumbled
- 4 ounces cream cheese, softened
- 2 tablespoons extra-virgin olive oil
- 1/8-1/4 teaspoon cayenne pepper (depending on your taste)
- 1/4 cup chopped sun-dried tomato
- 1/4 cup chopped Kalamata olive
- 1/2 teaspoon dried Mediterranean oregano, crumbled
- 1 small garlic clove, minced
- 1/2 cup walnuts, toasted, chopped
- 1/4 cup fresh parsley, minced

Directions:
1. With a mixer, combine the feta cheese, cream cheese, and the olive oil on medium speed until well combined. Add the remaining ingredients and mix well.
2. Shape the soft mixture into a 10-inch long log.

3. Combine the parsley and the walnuts; roll the log over the mixture, pressing slightly to stick the parsley and the walnuts on the sides of the log.

4. Wrap the log with plastic wrap; refrigerate for at least 5 hours to let the flavors blend.

5. Remove the plastic wrap, lay the log on a parsley-lined serving platter. Serve with whole-wheat crackers and toasted whole-wheat slices of baguette.

Nutrition Info:
- per serving:1154 cal., 106.3 g total fat (43.9 sat. fat), 226.2 mg chol., 2395.3 mg sodium, 23 g total carbs., 5 g fiber, 13.5 g sugar, and 35.2 g protein.

Avocado Dip

Servings: 8
Cooking Time: 0 Minutes

Ingredients:
- ½ cup heavy cream
- 1 green chili pepper, chopped
- Salt and pepper to the taste
- 4 avocados, pitted, peeled and chopped
- 1 cup cilantro, chopped
- ¼ cup lime juice

Directions:
1. In a blender, combine the cream with the avocados and the rest of the ingredients and pulse well.
2. Divide the mix into bowls and serve cold as a party dip.

Nutrition Info:
- calories 200, fat 14.5, fiber 3.8, carbs 8.1, protein 7.6

Stuffed Mushrooms

Servings:12
Cooking Time:20 Minutes

Ingredients:
- 12 large mushrooms, cleaned, hollowed out
- 2 tablespoons tomatoes, seeded, minced
- 2 tablespoons roasted red peppers, minced
- 2 tablespoons Kalamata olives, rinsed, minced
- 2 fresh garlic cloves, minced
- 1 tablespoon fresh parsley, minced
- 1/2 to 1 teaspoon oregano, minced (fresh or dry)
- 1 teaspoon fresh lemon juice
- 2 teaspoons olive oil
- 1/2 cup feta, crumbled
- Fresh ground black pepper, to taste
- Minced fresh parsley, to serve

Directions:
1. Preheat oven to 350F.
2. Lightly grease a 9x13-inch cookie sheet or baking dish.
3. Except for the mushrooms and the parsley, combine the rest of the ingredients. Spoon the filling into each hollowed mushroom caps. Place the stuffed mushrooms into the prepared baking dish; bake for about 20 to 25 minutes.

4. Place in the serving platter, sprinkle with the parsley, and serve.

Nutrition Info:
- Per Serving:31.4 cal., 2.3 g total fat (1.1 g sat fat), 5.6 mg chol., 101.1 mg sodium, 1.4 g total carbs., 0.3 g fiber, 0.8 g sugar, and 1.7 g protein.

Mediterranean Cheese Spread

Servings:1
Cooking Time: 15 Minutes

Ingredients:
- 8 ounces cream cheese, softened
- 3 tablespoons Kalamata olives, chopped
- 3 tablespoons fresh basil, chopped
- 2 tablespoons oil-packed sun-dried tomatoes, chopped
- 1/2 cup feta cheese, crumbled (about 2 ounces)
- 1 -2 clove garlic, minced

Directions:
1. Combine all of the ingredients; cover and chill for at least 1 hour or up to 24 hours.

Nutrition Info:
- Per Serving:702.9 cal., 66.5 g total fat (41.1 sat. fat), 210.8 mg chol., 1177 mg sodium, 10.2 g total carbs., 1.3 g fiber, 2.4 g sugar, and 19.4 g protein.

Cucumber Rolls

Servings: 6
Cooking Time: 0 Minutes

Ingredients:
- 1 big cucumber, sliced lengthwise
- 1 tablespoon parsley, chopped
- 8 ounces canned tuna, drained and mashed
- Salt and black pepper to the taste
- 1 teaspoon lime juice

Directions:
1. Arrange cucumber slices on a working surface, divide the rest of the ingredients, and roll.
2. Arrange all the rolls on a platter and serve as an appetizer.

Nutrition Info:
- calories 200, fat 6, fiber 3.4, carbs 7.6, protein 3.5

Chickpeas And Eggplant Bowls

Servings: 4
Cooking Time: 10 Minutes

Ingredients:
- 2 eggplants, cut in half lengthwise and cubed
- 1 red onion, chopped
- Juice of 1 lime
- 1 tablespoon olive oil
- 28 ounces canned chickpeas, drained and rinsed
- 1 bunch parsley, chopped
- A pinch of salt and black pepper
- 1 tablespoon balsamic vinegar

Directions:
1. Spread the eggplant cubes on a baking sheet lined with parchment paper, drizzle half of the oil all over, season with salt and pepper and cook at 425 degrees F for 10 minutes.
2. Cool the eggplant down, add the rest of the ingredients, toss, divide between appetizer plates and serve.

Nutrition Info:
- calories 263, fat 12, fiber 9.3, carbs 15.4, protein 7.5

Spinach Artichoke Dip

Servings:6
Cooking Time: 10 Minutes

Ingredients:
- 1 cup sour cream
- 1 cup fresh spinach
- 4 oz artichoke hearts, drained
- 1 cup Mozzarella cheese, shredded
- 1 teaspoon chili flakes

Directions:
1. Chop the artichoke hearts on the tiny pieces.
2. Put spinach in a blender and blend until smooth.
3. Mix up together spinach with artichokes. Add sour cream, Mozzarella cheese, and chili flakes. Stir well.
4. Transfer the mixture in the mold/pan and flatten it.
5. Bake the dip for 10 minutes at 360F.

Nutrition Info:
- Per Servingcalories 105, fat 8.9, fiber 1.1, carbs 4, protein 3.3

Slow Cooked Cheesy Artichoke Dip

Servings: 6
Cooking Time: 60 Minutes

Ingredients:
- 10 oz can artichoke hearts, drained and chopped
- 4 cups spinach, chopped
- 8 oz cream cheese
- 3 tbsp sour cream
- 1/4 cup mayonnaise
- 3/4 cup mozzarella cheese, shredded
- 1/4 cup parmesan cheese, grated
- 3 garlic cloves, minced
- 1/2 tsp dried parsley
- Pepper
- Salt

Directions:
1. Add all ingredients into the inner pot of instant pot and stir well.
2. Seal the pot with the lid and select slow cook mode and set the timer for 60 minutes. Stir once while cooking.
3. Serve and enjoy.

Nutrition Info:
- Calories 226 Fat 19.3 g Carbohydrates 7.5 g Sugar 1.2 g Protein 6.8 g Cholesterol 51 mg

Spinach Pies

Serves: 1 Pie
Cooking Time:20 Minutes

Ingredients:
- 8 cups baby spinach, washed and chopped
- 1 tsp. salt
- 1/4 cup plus 4 TB. extra-virgin olive oil
- 1 large tomato, finely diced
- 1 large yellow onion, finely chopped
- 1/4 cup fresh lemon juice
- 1/4 tsp. cayenne
- 1 tsp. sumac
- 1 batch Multipurpose Dough (recipe later in this chapter)

Directions:
1. In a large bowl, combine spinach and salt. Set aside for 20 minutes.
2. Preheat the oven to 400°F. Grease a baking sheet with 2 tablespoons extra-virgin olive oil.
3. Drain spinach and squeeze to remove any excess liquid. Place spinach in a separate large bowl.
4. Add tomato, yellow onion, lemon juice, 1/4 cup extra-virgin olive oil, cayenne, and sumac to spinach, and mix well.
5. Dust a rolling pin and counter with all-purpose flour, and roll out 18 Multipurpose Dough balls to 5-inch discs 1/4 inch thick.
6. Add 2 tablespoons spinach mixture to center of dough discs. Fold over and pinch together top portion halfway down. Bring up the bottom half, and pinch to top two halves. This should form a triangle.
7. Place spinach pies on the prepared baking sheet. Brush top of pies with remaining 2 tablespoons extra-virgin olive oil.
8. Bake for 18 to 20 minutes or until lightly browned.
9. Serve warm or cold.

Beet Spread

Servings:4
Cooking Time: 35 Minutes

Ingredients:
- 1 tablespoon pumpkin puree
- 1 beet, peeled
- 1 teaspoon tahini paste
- ½ teaspoon sesame seeds
- 1 teaspoon paprika
- 1 tablespoon olive oil
- ¼ cup water, boiled
- 1 tablespoon lime juice
- ½ teaspoon salt

Directions:
1. Place beet in the oven and bake it at 375F for 35 minutes.
2. Then chop it roughly and put in the food processor.
3. Blend the beet until smooth.
4. After this, add tahini paste, pumpkin puree, paprika, olive oil, water, lime juice, and salt.
5. Blend the hummus until smooth and fluffy.
6. Then transfer the appetizer in the bowl and sprinkle with sesame seeds.

Nutrition Info:
- Per Servingcalories 99, fat 8.6, fiber 1.6, carbs 3.9, protein 2.1

Eggplant Dip

Servings: 4
Cooking Time: 40 Minutes

Ingredients:
- 1 eggplant, poked with a fork
- 2 tablespoons tahini paste
- 2 tablespoons lemon juice
- 2 garlic cloves, minced
- 1 tablespoon olive oil
- Salt and black pepper to the taste
- 1 tablespoon parsley, chopped

Directions:
1. Put the eggplant in a roasting pan, bake at 400 degrees F for 40 minutes, cool down, peel and transfer to your food processor.
2. Add the rest of the ingredients except the parsley, pulse well, divide into small bowls and serve as an appetizer with the parsley sprinkled on top.

Nutrition Info:
- calories 121, fat 4.3, fiber 1, carbs 1.4, protein 4.3

Cucumber Bites

Servings: 12
Cooking Time: 0 Minutes

Ingredients:
- 1 English cucumber, sliced into 32 rounds
- 10 ounces hummus
- 16 cherry tomatoes, halved
- 1 tablespoon parsley, chopped
- 1 ounce feta cheese, crumbled

Directions:
1. Spread the hummus on each cucumber round, divide the tomato halves on each, sprinkle the cheese and parsley on to and serve as an appetizer.

Nutrition Info:
- calories 162, fat 3.4, fiber 2, carbs 6.4, protein 2.4

Creamy Artichoke Dip

Servings: 8
Cooking Time: 5 Minutes

Ingredients:
- 28 oz can artichoke hearts, drain and quartered
- 1 1/2 cups parmesan cheese, shredded
- 1 cup sour cream
- 1 cup mayonnaise
- 3.5 oz can green chilies
- 1 cup of water
- Pepper
- Salt

Directions:
1. Add artichokes, water, and green chilis into the instant pot.
2. Seal pot with the lid and select manual and set timer for 1 minute.
3. Once done, release pressure using quick release. Remove lid. Drain excess water.
4. Set instant pot on sauté mode. Add remaining ingredients and stir well and cook until cheese is melted.
5. Serve and enjoy.

Nutrition Info:
- Calories 262 Fat 7.6 g Carbohydrates 14.4 g Sugar 2.8 g Protein 8.4 g Cholesterol 32 mg

Vegetable Recipes

Vegetable Recipes

Hoemade Egg Drop Soup

Servings: 4
Cooking Time: 15 Minutes

Ingredients:
- 1 tbsp cornstarch
- 1 tbsp dried minced onion
- 1 tsp dried parsley
- 2 eggs
- 4 cubes chicken bouillon
- 4 cups water
- 1 cup chopped carrots
- ½ cup thinly shredded cabbage

Directions:
1. Combine water, bouillon, parsley, cabbage, carrots, and onion flakes in a saucepan, and then bring to a boil.
2. Beat the eggs lightly and stir into the soup.
3. Dissolve cornstarch with a little water. Stir until smooth and stir into the soup. Let it boil until the soup thickens.

Nutrition Info:
- Calories per serving: 98; Carbs: 6.9g; Protein: 5.1g; Fat: 5.3g

Mediterranean Diet Styled Stuffed Peppers

Servings: 4
Cooking Time: 30 Minutes

Ingredients:
- A handful of parsley, chopped roughly
- 0.40 lb. of feta cheese, crumbled finely
- 1 lb. of ready to eat quinoa
- 1 courgette, thinly sliced and quartered lengthwise
- 4 red peppers

Directions:
1. Preheat oven to 400oF.
2. Cut the peppers one by one lengthways and place on baking pan with the hollow side up. Remove and discard the seeds, season and drizzle with a tbsp. of olive oil. For fifteen minutes, roast the pepper.
3. In a fry pan, heat a tsp of olive oil and sauté the courgette. Before adding the parsley, feta and quinoa, remove fry pan from fire, season with pepper and mix well.
4. Then equally put the quinoa mixture into the hollow of the pepper and bake again in the oven for five more minutes.
5. Serve and enjoy while hot.

Nutrition Info:
- Calories per Serving: 294; Carbs: 34.2g; Protein: 13.4g; Fat: 12.2g

Collard Green Wrap Greek Style

Servings: 4
Cooking Time: 0 Minutes

Ingredients:
- ½ block feta, cut into 4 (1-inch thick) strips (4-oz)
- ½ cup purple onion, diced
- ½ medium red bell pepper, julienned
- 1 medium cucumber, julienned
- 4 large cherry tomatoes, halved
- 4 large collard green leaves, washed
- 8 whole kalamata olives, halved
- 1 cup full-fat plain Greek yogurt
- 1 tablespoon white vinegar
- 1 teaspoon garlic powder
- 2 tablespoons minced fresh dill
- 2 tablespoons olive oil
- 2.5-ounces cucumber, seeded and grated (¼-whole)
- Salt and pepper to taste

Directions:
1. Make the Tzatziki sauce first: make sure to squeeze out all the excess liquid from the cucumber after grating. In a small bowl, mix all sauce ingredients thoroughly and refrigerate.
2. Prepare and slice all wrap ingredients.
3. On a flat surface, spread one collard green leaf. Spread 2 tablespoons of Tzatziki sauce on middle of the leaf.
4. Layer ¼ of each of the tomatoes, feta, olives, onion, pepper, and cucumber. Place them on the center of the leaf, like piling them high instead of spreading them.
5. Fold the leaf like you would a burrito. Repeat process for remaining ingredients.
6. Serve and enjoy.

Nutrition Info:
- Calories per serving: 165.3; Protein: 7.0g; Carbs: 9.9g; Fat: 11.2g

Parsnips With Eggplant

Servings: 4
Cooking Time: 12 Minutes

Ingredients:

- 2 parsnips, sliced
- 1 cup can tomatoes, crushed
- 1/2 tsp ground cumin
- 1 tbsp paprika
- 1 tsp garlic, minced
- 1 eggplant, cut into chunks
- 1/4 tsp dried basil
- Pepper
- Salt

Directions:

1. Add all ingredients into the instant pot and stir well.
2. Seal pot with lid and cook on high for 12 minutes.
3. Once done, release pressure using quick release. Remove lid.
4. Stir and serve.

Nutrition Info:

- Calories 98 0.7 g Carbohydrates 23 g Sugar 8.8 g Protein 2.8 g Cholesterol 0 mg

Feta And Roasted Eggplant Dip

Servings: 12
Cooking Time: 20 Minutes

Ingredients:

- ¼ tsp salt
- ¼ tsp cayenne pepper
- 1 tbsp finely chopped flat leaf parsley
- 2 tbsp chopped fresh basil
- 1 small Chile pepper
- 1 small red bell pepper, finely chopped
- ½ cup finely chopped red onion
- ½ cup crumbled Greek nonfat feta cheese
- ¼ cup extra-virgin olive oil
- 2 tbsp lemon juice
- 1 medium eggplant, around 1 lb.

Directions:

1. Preheat broiler, position rack on topmost part of oven, and line a baking pan with foil.
2. With a fork or knife, poke eggplant, place on prepared baking pan, and broil for 5 minutes per side until skin is charred all around.
3. Once eggplant skin is charred, remove from broiler and allow to cool to handle.
4. Once eggplant is cool enough to handle, slice in half lengthwise, scoop out flesh, and place in a medium bowl.
5. Pour in lemon juice and toss eggplant to coat with lemon juice and prevent it from discoloring.
6. Add oil; continue mixing until oil is absorbed by eggplant.
7. Stir in salt, cayenne pepper, parsley, basil, Chile pepper, bell pepper, onion, and feta.
8. Toss to mix well and serve.

Nutrition Info:

- Calories per Serving: 58; Carbs: 3.7g; Protein: 1.2g; Fat: 4.6g

Cardamom And Carrot Soup

Servings: 4
Cooking Time: 45 Minutes

Ingredients:

- Freshly ground black pepper
- ½ cup full-fat coconut milk
- 4 cups chicken stock or Bone Broth
- ½ teaspoon ground cardamom
- 1 teaspoon minced fresh ginger
- ¼ cup diced Cortland apple, Empire, McIntosh, or Braeburn
- 1 ½ pounds peeled large carrots, cut into ½ inch coins
- Kosher Salt
- 2 large green onions, green and white ends only, trimmed and cleaned, and thinly sliced
- 1 tablespoon coconut oil

Directions:

1. On medium fire, place large saucepan and heat coconut oil.
2. Sauté salt and leeks for 5 minutes or until translucent.
3. Add cardamom, ginger, apple, and carrot. Sauté for 3 minutes.
4. Add broth and boil on high fire.
5. When boiling, lower heat to a simmer, cover, and cook for 30 minutes or until carrots and apples are soft.
6. Add coconut milk, turn off fire, and mix.
7. With an immersion blender, puree soup.
8. Season to taste with pepper and salt.
9. Serve while warm.

Nutrition Info:

- Calories per Serving: 185; Carbs: 20.6g; Protein: 3.1g; Fat: 11.6g

Basil Corn

Servings:5
Cooking Time: 20 Minutes

Ingredients:

- 5 corn on cobs
- 5 teaspoons olive oil
- ¼ teaspoon dried oregano
- 1/3 teaspoon ground black pepper
- 5 teaspoons Plain yogurt
- 1 tablespoon fresh basil, chopped

Directions:

1. Mix up together olive oil, dried oregano, and ground black pepper.
2. Place the corn on the cobs on the foil and brush with the olive oil mixture.
3. Wrap the corn on the cobs in the foil and grill at 395F for20 minutes. Flip the wrapped corn on the cobs every five minutes.
4. Remove the foil from the corn on the cobs and sprinkle with Plain yogurt and fresh basil.

Nutrition Info:
- Per Servingcalories 215, fat 7.4, fiber 3.7, carbs 33.7, protein 0.3

Sage Artichokes

Servings:4
Cooking Time: 5 Minutes

Ingredients:
- 3 fresh artichokes
- 1/3 cup almond flour
- 3 eggs, beaten
- 1 teaspoon dried basil
- ¼ teaspoon sage
- 1/3 teaspoon salt
- 4 tablespoons coconut oil

Directions:
1. Trim the artichoke and separate them on the petals.
2. In the mixing bowl mix up together almond flour, dried basil, sage, and salt.
3. Then dip artichoke petals in the egg mixture.
4. After this, coat every artichoke petal in the almond flour.
5. Toss the coconut oil in the small saucepan and bring it to boil.
6. Carefully put the coated artichoke petals in the hot coconut oil and roast them for 1 minute or until they are crunchy and light brown.

Nutrition Info:
- Per Servingcalories 235, fat 18.2, fiber 6.8, carbs 13.6, protein 8.6

Zucchini Tomato Potato Ratatouille

Servings: 6
Cooking Time: 10 Minutes

Ingredients:
- 1 1/2 lbs potatoes, cut into cubes
- 1/2 cup fresh basil
- 28 oz fire-roasted tomatoes, chopped
- 1 onion, chopped
- 4 mushrooms, sliced
- 1 bell pepper, diced
- 12 oz eggplant, diced
- 8 oz zucchini, diced
- 8 oz yellow squash, diced

- Pepper
- Salt

Directions:
1. Add all ingredients except basil into the instant pot and stir well.
2. Seal pot with lid and cook on high for 10 minutes.
3. Once done, release pressure using quick release. Remove lid.
4. Add basil and stir well and serve.

Nutrition Info:
- Calories 175 Fat 1.9 g Carbohydra

Chili Lentils

Servings:6
Cooking Time: 20 Minutes

Ingredients:
- 1 cup lentils
- 2.5 cups water
- 1 tablespoon olive oil
- 1 teaspoon salt
- 3 tablespoons butter
- 1 teaspoon chili powder

Directions:
1. Heat up olive oil in the pan.
2. Add lentils and roast them for 3 minutes over the medium heat. Stir them constantly.
3. Then add water and salt.
4. Close the lid and boil the lentils for 15 minutes.
5. After this, add chili powder and butter.
6. Stir the lentils until the butter is melted.
7. Chill the meal to the room temperature and put in the bowls.

Nutrition Info:
- Per Servingcalories 185, fat 8.5, fiber 9.9, carbs 19.5, protein 8.4

Mediterranean Grilled Cheese Sandwiches

Serves: 1 Sandwich
Cooking Time:8 Minutes

Ingredients:
- 8 pieces rustic loaf bread
- 8 oz. Brie cheese, cut into 8 slices
- 4 slices Havarti cheese
- 1/2 cup fresh basil, finely chopped
- 1/2 cup sun-dried tomatoes, finely chopped
- 1 tsp. ground black pepper
- 4 slices Colby jack cheese
- 4 TB. extra-virgin olive oil

Directions:
1. Place 4 slices bread on your work surface, top each slice

with 2 slices of Brie cheese and 1 slice Havarti cheese.

2. Evenly divide basil and sun-dried tomato among sandwiches, sprinkle with ground black pepper, and top with 1 slice of Colby jack cheese each. Cover each sandwich with remaining slices of bread.

3. Preheat a large skillet or griddle over medium heat. Add 2 tablespoons extra-virgin olive oil, and cook sandwiches for 4 minutes on one side.

4. Drizzle remaining 2 tablespoons extra-virgin olive oil over sandwiches, flip them over, and cook for 4 more minutes.

5. Remove from heat, and serve warm.

Vegetarian Stuffed Baked Potatoes

Serves: 1 Potato
Cooking Time:38 Minutes

Ingredients:
- 6 large potatoes, peeled
- 1 lb. baby spinach, chopped
- 2 cups broccoli florets, finely chopped
- 1 large yellow onion, finely chopped
- 2 TB. minced garlic
- 4 TB. extra-virgin olive oil
- 2 tsp. salt
- 1 TB. seven spices
- 1 (16-oz.) can plain tomato sauce
- 1 TB. fresh thyme
- 1 tsp. dried oregano
- 1 tsp. ground black pepper
- 1/2 tsp. garlic powder

Directions:
1. Preheat the oven to 450°F.
2. Trim bottom of potatoes so they stand on end. Cut off top quarter of potatoes, and set aside tops. Hollow out inside of potatoes, and stand potatoes in a large casserole dish. Finely chop potato flesh, and set aside.
3. In a large skillet over medium heat, cook spinach for 3 minutes.
4. Add broccoli, yellow onion, garlic, 2 tablespoons extra-virgin olive oil, 1 teaspoon salt, seven spices, and chopped potato flesh, and cook for 5 minutes.
5. Fill each potato with 3 tablespoons vegetable mixture, and place tops back on filled potatoes. Evenly drizzle remaining 2 tablespoons extra-virgin olive oil over potatoes, and bake for 15 minutes.
6. In a 2-quart pot over medium heat, combine tomato sauce, remaining 1 teaspoon salt, thyme, oregano, black pepper, and garlic powder, and simmer for 10 minutes.
7. After potatoes have baked for 15 minutes, add sauce mixture to the dish, and bake for 15 more minutes.
8. Remove from the oven, and serve warm.

Thyme Mushrooms

Servings:3
Cooking Time: 20 Minutes

Ingredients:
- 3 Portobello mushroom caps
- ½ teaspoon thyme
- ¼ teaspoon salt
- 4 teaspoons butter

Directions:
1. Place the mushroom caps in the tray and sprinkle them with salt and thyme.
2. Then fill the mushrooms with butter.
3. Bake Portobello caps for 20 minutes at 355F.

Nutrition Info:
- Per Servingcalories 65, fat 5.1, fiber 1.1, carbs 3.1, protein 3.1

Provolone Over Herbed Portobello Mushrooms

Servings: 2
Cooking Time: 10 Minutes

Ingredients:
- ¼ cup grated provolone cheese
- 1 tsp minced garlic
- ¼ tsp dried rosemary
- 1 tbsp brown sugar
- ½ cup balsamic vinegar
- 2 Portobello mushrooms, stemmed and wiped clean

Directions:
1. In oven, position rack 4-inches away from the top and preheat broiler.
2. Prepare a baking dish by spraying with cooking spray lightly.
3. Stemless, place mushroom gill side up.
4. Mix well garlic, rosemary, brown sugar and vinegar in a small bowl.
5. Drizzle over mushrooms equally.
6. Marinate for at least 5 minutes before popping into the oven and broiling for 4 minutes per side or until tender.
7. Once cooked, remove from oven, sprinkle cheese, return to broiler and broil for a minute or two or until cheese melts.
8. Remove from oven and serve right away.

Nutrition Info:
- Calories per Serving: 168; Carbs: 21.5g; Protein: 8.6g; Fat: 5.1g

Soy Eggplants

Servings:4
Cooking Time: 8 Minutes

Ingredients:
- 3 eggplants, trimmed
- 1 teaspoon minced garlic
- 1 tablespoon mustard
- 1 tablespoon olive oil
- 1 tablespoon lemon juice
- 1 teaspoon dried oregano
- ½ teaspoon soy sauce
- ½ teaspoon dried thyme
- ½ teaspoon ground black pepper

Directions:
1. Cut the eggplants lengthwise and then cut them on 3 lengthwise pieces more.
2. Mix up together minced garlic, mustard, olive oil, lemon juice, dried oregano, soy sauce, dried thyme, and ground black pepper.
3. Brush the eggplants with mustard mixture well.
4. Preheat the grill to 400F.
5. Place the eggplants in the grill and cook them for 4 minutes from each side.

Nutrition Info:
- Per Servingcalories 150, fat 5.1, fiber 15.2, carbs 26, protein 4.9

Instant Pot Artichoke Hearts

Servings: 6
Cooking Time: 30 Minutes

Ingredients:
- 4 artichokes, rinsed and trimmed
- Juice from 2 small lemons, freshly squeezed
- 2 cups bone broth
- 1 tablespoon tarragon leaves
- 1 stalk, celery
- ½ cup extra virgin olive oil
- Salt and pepper to taste

Directions:
1. Place all ingredients in a pressure cooker.
2. Give a good stir.
3. Close the lid and seal the valve.
4. Pressure cook for 4 minutes.
5. Allow pressure cooker to release steam naturally.
6. Then serve and enjoy.

Nutrition Info:
- Calories per serving: 133; Carbs: 14.3g; Protein: 4.4g; Fat: 11.7g

Zucchini Fritters

Serves: 1 Fritter
Cooking Time:10 Minutes

Ingredients:
- 2 large zucchini, grated
- 3 whole green onions, finely chopped
- 1/4 cup fresh Italian parsley, finely chopped
- 1 tsp. dried mint
- 1/2 tsp. cayenne
- 1 tsp. salt
- 1/2 tsp. ground black pepper
- 2 large eggs
- 1/2 cup all-purpose flour
- 3 TB. water
- 1 cup extra-virgin olive oil

Directions:
1. In a large bowl, combine zucchini, green onions, Italian parsley, mint, cayenne, salt, black pepper, eggs, all-purpose flour, and water.
2. In a 3-quart pot or fryer over high heat, heat extra-virgin olive oil to 325ºF.
3. Drop batter into the fryer with a large tablespoon, and fry for 3 minutes per side or until golden brown. Do not overcrowd the pot. Remove fritters from the pot, and place on a plate lined with paper towels. Serve immediately.

Coconut Squash Flowers

Servings:4
Cooking Time: 5 Minutes

Ingredients:
- 4 oz squash blossoms
- ½ cup of sparkling water
- 2 tablespoons wheat flour, whole grain
- 1 teaspoon cornstarch
- 3 tablespoons coconut oil
- ½ teaspoon salt

Directions:
1. In the mixing bowl mix up together sparkling water, flour, cornstarch, and salt.
2. When the liquid is smooth dip the squash blossoms in it.
3. Bring the coconut oil to boiling.
4. Put the dipped squash blossoms in the hot oil and roast them for 1 minute from each side.
5. Dry the cooked blossoms with the help of the paper towel and transfer in the serving plates.

Nutrition Info:
- Per Servingcalories 109, fat 10.2, fiber 0.1, carbs 4.5, protein 0.4

Sweet Potatoes Oven Fried

Servings: 7
Cooking Time: 30 Minutes

Ingredients:

- 1 small garlic clove, minced
- 1 tsp grated orange rind
- 1 tbsp fresh parsley, chopped finely
- ¼ tsp pepper
- ¼ tsp salt
- 1 tbsp olive oil
- 4 medium sweet potatoes, peeled and sliced to ¼-inch thickness

Directions:

1. In a large bowl mix well pepper, salt, olive oil and sweet potatoes.
2. In a greased baking sheet, in a single layer arrange sweet potatoes.
3. Pop in a preheated 400oF oven and bake for 15 minutes, turnover potato slices and return to oven. Bake for another 15 minutes or until tender.
4. Meanwhile, mix well in a small bowl garlic, orange rind and parsley, sprinkle over cooked potato slices and serve.
5. You can store baked sweet potatoes in a lidded container and just microwave whenever you want to eat it. Do consume within 3 days.

Nutrition Info:

- Calories per Serving: 176; Carbs: 36.6g; Protein: 2.5g; Fat: 2.5g

Vegetarian Potato Kibbeh

Serves: 1/6 Of Casserole
Cooking Time:40 Minutes

Ingredients:

- 1 cup bulgur wheat, grind #1
- 1 cup warm water
- 4 large boiled potatoes, peeled
- 1/2 cup all-purpose flour
- 21/2 tsp. salt
- 1/2 tsp. allspice
- 1/2 tsp. cumin
- 1/2 tsp. ground coriander
- 1/2 tsp. ground nutmeg
- 1/2 tsp. ground cloves
- 1/2 tsp. ground cinnamon
- 1/2 tsp. cayenne
- 1 tsp. ground black pepper
- 1/4 cup plus 2 TB. extra-virgin olive oil
- 1/2 medium red bell pepper
- 1/2 medium green bell pepper
- 1/2 medium yellow onion
- 1/2 cup pine nuts
- 1/2 cup walnuts
- 1 tsp. seven spices
- 1 tsp. sumac

Directions:

1. In a large bowl, combine bulgur wheat and warm water, and set aside for 20 minutes.
2. Add potatoes, all-purpose flour, 2 teaspoons salt, allspice, cumin, coriander, nutmeg, cloves, cinnamon, cayenne, and black pepper, and knead together for about 4 or 5 minutes until well combined. Set aside.
3. In a medium skillet over medium heat, heat 1/4 cup extra-virgin olive oil. Add red bell pepper, green bell pepper, and onions, and cook for 5 minutes.
4. Stir in remaining 1/2 teaspoon salt, pine nuts, walnuts, seven spices, and sumac, and cook for 3 minutes.
5. Preheat the oven to 450°F. Grease an 8×8-inch baking dish with extra-virgin olive oil.
6. Divide kibbeh dough in half, and spread a layer of kibbeh dough on the bottom of the baking dish. Add a layer of sautéed vegetables and top with another layer of kibbeh dough.
7. Paint top of kibbeh with remaining 2 tablespoons extra-virgin olive oil, and cut kibbeh into 6 equal pieces. Bake for 30 minutes.
8. Let kibbeh rest for 15 minutes before serving.

Avocado Salad

Servings:2
Cooking Time: 0 Minutes

Ingredients:

- 1 ½ cup arugula, chopped
- 1 avocado, chopped
- 1 cucumber, chopped
- ½ lemon
- ½ teaspoon ground black pepper

Directions:

1. Combine together arugula, avocado, and cucumber in the salad bowl.
2. Squeeze the lemon juice over the salad and sprinkle it with ground black pepper.
3. Mix up the salad well.

Nutrition Info:

- Per Servingcalories 237, fat 19.9, fiber 8.3, carbs 16.3, protein 3.5

Almond Kale

Servings:2
Cooking Time: 10 Minutes

Ingredients:
- 2 cups kale, chopped
- 1 tablespoon butter
- 1 cup of water
- 1 tablespoon almond, chopped
- 1 teaspoon cumin seeds
- ½ teaspoon salt

Directions:
1. Bring the water to boil.
2. Add kale in the hot water and boil the greens for 3 minutes.
3. After this, drain the water.
4. Melt the butter in the skillet.
5. Add cumin seeds and roast them for 1 minute over the medium heat or until they start to give a smell.
6. Add boiled kale and mix up.
7. After this, sprinkle the kale with salt and almonds. Mix up well.
8. Roast the kale for 2 minutes.

Nutrition Info:
- Per Servingcalories 105, fat 7.5, fiber 1.5, carbs 8.1, protein 2.9

Summer Veggies In Instant Pot

Servings: 6
Cooking Time: 7 Minutes

Ingredients:
- 2 cups okra, sliced
- 1 cup grape tomatoes
- 1 cup mushroom, sliced
- 1 ½ cups onion, sliced
- 2 cups bell pepper, sliced
- 2 ½ cups zucchini, sliced
- 2 tablespoons basil, chopped
- 1 tablespoon thyme, chopped
- ½ cups balsamic vinegar
- ½ cups olive oil
- Salt and pepper

Directions:
1. Place all ingredients in the Instant Pot.
2. Stir the contents and close the lid.
3. Close the lid and press the Manual button.
4. Adjust the cooking time to 7 minutes.
5. Do quick pressure release.
6. Once cooled, evenly divide into serving size, keep in your preferred container, and refrigerate until ready to eat.

Nutrition Info:
- Calories per serving:233; Carbs: 7g; Protein: 3g; Fat: 18g

Lunch & Dinner Recipes

Minted Roasted Leg Of Lamb

Servings: 10
Cooking Time:2 ¼ Hours

Ingredients:

- 4 pounds leg of lamb
- 4 mint leaves, chopped
- 1 teaspoon dried oregano
- ½ cup chopped parsley
- 6 garlic cloves, minced
- 3 tablespoons olive oil
- 1 tablespoon lemon zest
- Salt and pepper to taste

Directions:

1. Season the lamb with salt and pepper.
2. Mix the mint, oregano, parsley, garlic, oil and lemon zest in a bowl.
3. Spread the mixture over the lamb and place it in a deep dish baking pan.
4. Cover with aluminum foil and cook in the preheated oven at 300F for 1 ½ hours.
5. Remove the foil and continue cooking for another 30 minutes at 350F.
6. Serve the lamb warm and fresh.

Nutrition Info:

- Per Serving:Calories:380 Fat:17.6g Protein:51.3g Carbohydrates:1.4g

Ground Pork And Tomatoes Soup

Servings: 4
Cooking Time: 40 Minutes

Ingredients:

- 1 pound pork meat, ground
- Salt and black pepper to the taste
- 2 garlic cloves, minced
- 2 teaspoons thyme, dried
- 2 tablespoons olive oil
- 4 cups beef stock
- A pinch of saffron powder
- 15 ounces canned tomatoes, crushed
- 1 tablespoons parsley, chopped

Directions:

1. Heat up a pot with the oil over medium heat, add the meat and the garlic and brown for 5 minutes.
2. Add the rest of the ingredients except the parsley, bring to a simmer and cook for 25 minutes.
3. Divide the soup into bowls, sprinkle the parsley on top and serve.

Nutrition Info:

- calories 372, fat 17.3, fiber 5

Quinoa Zuc

Servings: 6
Cooking Time:50 Minutes

Ingredients:

- 2 tablespoons olive oil
- 1 shallot, chopped
- 2 garlic cloves, chopped
- 2 zucchinis, diced
- 2 tomatoes, peeled and diced
- ¾ cup quinoa, rinsed
- 2 cups vegetable stock
- 1 bay leaf
- Salt and pepper to taste

Directions:

1. Heat the oil in a skillet an Cook for 2 minutes.
2. Add the zucchinis, tomatoe minutes then pour in the stock.
3. Add the bay leaf, salt and utes.
4. Serve the stew warm and fr

Nutrition Info:

- Per Serving:Calories:141 Fa drates:18.5g

Quinoa Chick

Servings: 8
Cooking Time:1 ¼ Hours

Ingredients:

- ¾ cup quinoa, rinsed
- 1 carrot, diced
- 1 celery stalk, diced
- 1 shallot, chopped
- 1 red bell pepper, cored and
- 1 yellow bell pepper, cored a
- 2 garlic cloves, chopped
- 2 tomatoes, peeled and diced
- 4 chicken breasts, halved
- 1 rosemary sprig
- 2 cups chicken stock

Directions:

1. Combine the quinoa, carrot, garlic and tomatoes in a deep d
2. Pour in the stock then place

top.
3. Cover heated ov
4. Serve

Nutrition

- Per Se hydrates:

Servings:
Cooking T

Ingredie

- 3 tables
- 4 garlic
- 1 red or
- 1 celery
- 2 red be
- 2 tables
- 2 cups c
- 1 cup v
- Salt and
- 4 cod fi
- 4 sea ba
- 2 tables

Direction

1. Season flour.
2. Heat t all sides u not cooke
3. Remov
4. Add th the fish w
5. Stir in and peppe
6. Cook cook for a
7. Serve t

Nutrition

- Per Se hydrates:

Servings:
Cooking T

Ingredie

- 3 tables
- 1 sweet
- 2 garlic
- 1 celery
- 2 carrot
- 1 cup o

Medite

the pan with aluminum foil and cook in the pre-
n at 330F for 45 minutes.
e casserole warm and fresh.

Info:
ving:Calories:215 Fat:6.5g Protein:23.4g Carbo-
4.8g

Summer Fish Stew

me:1 Hour

ts:
oons olive oil
:loves, minced
on, chopped
stalk, sliced
l peppers, cored and diced
oons tomato paste
nerry tomatoes
getable stock
pepper to taste
ets, cubed
s fillets, cubed
oons all-purpose flour

:
the fish with salt and pepper then sprinkle it with

e oil in a skillet then place the fish and cook it on
til golden brown. It just has to be golden brown,
through just yet.
e the fish on a platter.
garlic, onion and celery in the same skillet as
s in and cook for 2 minutes until fragrant.
the remaining ingredients and season with salt

or 10 minutes on low heat then add the fish and
other 10 minutes.
e stew warm and fresh.

Info:
ving:Calories:318 Fat:10.1g Protein:45.1g Carbo-
).3g

Spinach Orzo Stew

me:1 Hour

s:
oons olive oil
onion, chopped
:loves, minced
stalk, diced
, diced
o, rinsed

- 2 cups vegetable stock
- Salt and pepper to taste
- 4 cups baby spinach
- 1 tablespoon lemon juice

Directions:
1. Heat the oil in a skillet and stir in the onion, garlic, celery and carrots. Cook for 2 minutes until softened then add
the orzo.
2. Cook for another 5 minutes then pour in the stock.
3. Add the salt and pepper and cook on low heat for 20
minutes.
4. Add the spinach and lemon juice and cook for another 5
minutes.
5. Serve the stew warm and fresh.

Nutrition Info:
- Per Serving:Calories:143 Fat:5.8g Protein:3.5g Carbohy-
drates:19.8g

Pistachio Crusted Lamb Chops

Servings: 6
Cooking Time:45 Minutes

Ingredients:
- 6 lamb chops
- 3 tablespoons olive oil
- 1 teaspoon chili powder
- 1 cup ground pistachios
- Salt and pepper to taste

Directions:
1. Season the lamb chops with salt, pepper and chili powder then drizzle with oil and rub it well into the meat.
2. Roll the meat chops into the ground pistachios and place
them in a baking tray.
3. Cook in the preheated oven at 350F for 20 minutes.
4. Serve the lamb chops warm and fresh.

Nutrition Info:
- Per Serving:Calories:185 Fat:12.0g Protein:18.8g Carbo-
hydrates:0.2g

Moroccan spices Crusted Sea Bass

Servings: 4
Cooking Time:12 Minutes

Ingredients:
- 4 (6-ounce) sea bass fillets (about 1 inch thick)
- 1 tablespoon olive oil
- Cilantro sprigs (optional)
- Lemon wedges (optional)
- 3 garlic cloves, crushed
- 1/4 teaspoon red pepper, crushed
- 1/4 cup lemon juice, freshly squeezed
- 1 teaspoon ground cumin
- 1 tablespoon fresh cilantro, minced

- 1 teaspoon caraway seeds
- 1 teaspoon ground cumin
- 1 teaspoon paprika
- 1/4 teaspoon of salt
- 2 tablespoons ground coriander
- 2 teaspoons black pepper (freshly ground)

Directions:

1. In a large-sized-sized Ziploc bag, combine the marinade ingredients together; add the fish into the bag, seal the bag, and marinate for 45 minutes in the refrigerator. When marinated, remove the fish from the bag; discard the marinade.

2. In a medium-sized bowl, combine the spice rub ingredients; rub and coat the fish with the mix.

3. In a large-sized-sized nonstick skillet, heat the oil over medium flame or heat. Add the fish and cook for about 6 minutes per side or until the flesh easily flakes when fork-tested. If desired, garnish with the cilantro and the lemon wedges.

Nutrition Info:

- Per Serving:20 Cal, 7.2 g total fat (1.4 g sat. fat, 3.4 g mono fat, 1.7 g poly fat), 32.1 g protein, 3.2 g carb., 0.7 g fiber, 70 mg chol., 2 mg iron, 267 mg sodium, and 48 mg calcium.

Chicken Zucchini Ragout

Servings: 8
Cooking Time:1 Hour

Ingredients:

- 3 tablespoons olive oil
- 2 pounds ground chicken
- 4 garlic cloves, minced
- 3 shallots, chopped
- 2 carrots, sliced
- 3 zucchinis, cubed
- 1 can diced tomatoes
- 1 cup chicken stock
- 2 tablespoons tomato paste
- 1 bay leaf
- 1 thyme sprig
- Salt and pepper to taste

Directions:

1. Heat the oil in a heavy saucepan and stir in the ground chicken. Cook for 5 minutes then add the garlic and shallots.

2. Cook for 5 minutes then stir in the rest of the ingredients.

3. Add enough salt and pepper then lower the heat and cook for 30 minutes.

4. Serve the ragout warm and fresh.

Nutrition Info:

- Per Serving:Calories:290 Fat:13.9g Protein:34.4g Carbohydrates:6.4g

Olive Oil Lemon Broiled Cod

Servings: 4
Cooking Time:35 Minutes

Ingredients:

- 4 cod fillets
- 1 teaspoon dried marjoram
- 4 tablespoons olive oil
- 1 lemon, juiced
- 1 thyme sprig
- Salt and pepper to taste

Directions:

1. Season the cod with salt, pepper and marjoram.

2. Heat the oil in a large skillet and place the cod in the hot oil.

3. Fry on medium heat on both sides until golden brown then add the lemon juice.

4. Place the thyme sprig on top and cover with a lid.

5. Cook for 5 more minutes then remove from heat.

6. Serve the cod and sauce fresh.

Nutrition Info:

- Per Serving:Calories:304 Fat:15.5g Protein:40.0g Carbohydrates:0.1g

Veggie Soup

Servings: 8
Cooking Time: 45 Minutes

Ingredients:

- 1 yellow onion, chopped
- 4 garlic cloves, minced
- ½ cup carrots, chopped
- 1 zucchini, chopped
- 1 yellow squash, peeled and cubed
- 2 tablespoons parsley, chopped
- 3 tablespoons olive oil
- ¼ cup celery, chopped
- 30 ounces canned cannellini beans, drained and rinsed
- 30 ounces canned red kidney beans, drained and rinsed
- 4 cups veggie stock
- 2 cups water
- ¼ teaspoon thyme, dried
- ½ teaspoon basil, dried
- A pinch of salt and black pepper
- 4 cups baby spinach
- ¼ cup parmesan, grated

Directions:

1. Heat up a pot with the oil over medium heat, add the onion, garlic, carrots, squash, zucchini, parsley and the celery, stir and sauté for 5 minutes.

2. Add the rest of the ingredients except the spinach and the parmesan, stir, bring to a simmer over medium heat and cook for 30 minutes.

3. Add the spinach, cook the soup for 10 minutes more, divide into bowls, sprinkle the cheese on top and serve.

Nutrition Info:
- calories 300, fat 11.3, fiber 3.4, carbs 17.5, protein 10

Lamb Soup

Servings: 8
Cooking Time: 50 Minutes

Ingredients:
- 1 ½-pound lamb bone in
- 4 eggs, beaten
- 2 cups lettuce, chopped
- 1 tablespoon chives, chopped
- ½ cup fresh dill, chopped
- ½ cup lemon juice
- 1 teaspoon salt
- ½ teaspoon white pepper
- 2 tablespoons avocado oil
- 5 cups of water

Directions:
1. Chop the lamb roughly and place in the pan.
2. Add avocado oil and roast the meat for 10 minutes over the medium heat. Stir it with the help of spatula from time to time.
3. Then sprinkle the meat with white pepper and salt. Add water and bring the mixture to boil.
4. In the mixing bowl, whisk together eggs and lemon juice.
5. Add a ½ cup of boiling water from the pan and whisk the egg mixture until smooth.
6. Add dill, chives, and lettuce in the soup. Stir well.
7. Cook the soup for 30 minutes over the medium-high heat.
8. Then add egg mixture and stir it fast to make the homogenous texture of the soup.
9. Cook it for 3 minutes more.

Nutrition Info:
- Per Servingcalories 360, fat 22.9, fiber 0.8, carbs 2.9, protein 33.6

Roasted Vegetables And Chorizo

Servings: 6
Cooking Time:1 Hour

Ingredients:
- 3 tablespoons olive oil
- 1 zucchini, sliced
- 1 egg plant, sliced
- 2 red bell peppers, cored and sliced
- 2 red beets, peeled and cubed
- 4 potatoes, peeled and cubed
- 2 tomatoes, sliced
- Salt and pepper to taste

- 1 teaspoon smoked paprika
- 1 Chorizo link, sliced
- 1 tablespoon balsamic vinegar

Directions:
1. Combine all the ingredients in a deep dish baking pan.
2. Adjust the taste with salt and pepper and cook in the preheated oven at 350F for 40 minutes.
3. Serve the vegetables warm and fresh.

Nutrition Info:
- Per Serving:Calories:242 Fat:11.3g Protein:6.5g Carbohydrates:30.6g

Spice-rubbed Beef Steaks

Servings: 4
Cooking Time:40 Minutes

Ingredients:
- 4 beef steaks
- 2 tablespoons dark brown sugar
- 1 teaspoon cumin powder
- ½ teaspoon chili powder
- ½ teaspoon garlic powder
- ½ teaspoon onion powder
- 1 teaspoon smoked paprika
- Salt and pepper to taste
- 2 tomatoes, peeled and diced
- 2 tablespoons chopped cilantro
- 1 red onion, sliced
- 1 cucumber, diced
- 1 teaspoon sherry vinegar

Directions:
1. Mix the sugar, cumin powder, chili, garlic powder, onion and paprika in a bowl. Add a pinch of salt and pepper as well.
2. Spread the spice rub on the steaks and rub them well.
3. Heat a grill pan over medium flame and place the steaks on the grill.
4. Cook on each side until browned.
5. Mix the tomatoes, cilantro, red onion, cucumber, vinegar, salt and pepper in a bowl.
6. Top the steaks with the vegetable mix and serve them fresh.

Nutrition Info:
- Per Serving:Calories:169 Fat:4.2g Protein:19.8g Carbohydrates:13.3g

Buttermilk Marinated Roast Chicken

Servings: 8
Cooking Time:4 Hours

Ingredients:
- 1 whole chicken
- 2 cups buttermilk
- 2 jalapenos, chopped
- 1 teaspoon Dijon mustard
- 1 teaspoon chili powder
- ½ cup chopped cilantro
- Salt and pepper to taste

Directions:
1. Combine all the ingredients in a zip lock bag.
2. Add salt and pepper to taste and place the chicken in the fridge for 2 hours.
3. Transfer the chicken in a deep dish baking pan and cover with aluminum foil.
4. Cook in the preheated oven at 300F for 1 ½ hours then remove the foil and continue cooking for 30 more minutes on 350F.
5. Serve the chicken warm and fresh with your favorite side dish.

Nutrition Info:
- Per Serving:Calories:121 Fat:3.9g Protein:14.4g Carbohydrates:6.8g

Tuna And Spinach Salad

Servings: 5
Cooking Time: 6 Minutes

Ingredients:
- 4 servings tuna fillet (3 oz each)
- 1 orange, peeled, chopped
- 1 tablespoon almond flakes
- ½ teaspoon chili flakes
- 1 teaspoon olive oil
- 1 teaspoon salt
- 1 teaspoon turmeric
- 3 cups Spinach, chopped
- 1 tablespoon lime juice
- 1 tablespoon avocado oil

Directions:
1. Sprinkle tuna fillets with salt, turmeric, and drizzle with olive oil.
2. Grill the fish for 3 minutes from each side at 365F.
3. Then chop the grilled fish roughly and put in the salad bowl.
4. Add almond flakes, spinach, lime juice, avocado oil, orange, chili flakes, and shake the salad well.

Nutrition Info:
- Per Servingcalories 337, fat 27.3, fiber 1.7, carbs 5.6, protein 18.1

Pork And Prunes Stew

Servings: 8
Cooking Time:1 ¼ Hours

Ingredients:
- 2 pounds pork tenderloin, cubed
- 2 tablespoons olive oil
- 1 sweet onions, chopped
- 4 garlic cloves, chopped
- 2 carrots, diced
- 2 celery stalks, chopped
- 2 tomatoes, peeled and diced
- 1 cup vegetable stock
- ½ cup white wine
- 1 pound prunes, pitted
- 1 bay leaf
- 1 thyme sprig
- 1 teaspoon mustard seeds
- 1 teaspoon coriander seeds
- Salt and pepper to taste

Directions:
1. Combine all the ingredients in a deep dish baking pan.
2. Add salt and pepper to taste and cook in the preheated oven at 350F for 1 hour, adding more liquid as it cooks if needed.
3. Serve the stew warm and fresh.

Nutrition Info:
- Per Serving:Calories:363 Fat:7.9g Protein:31.7g Carbohydrates:41.4g

Spicy Potato Salad

Servings: 4
Cooking Time: 15 Minutes

Ingredients:
- 1 and ½ pounds baby potatoes, peeled and halved
- A pinch of salt and black pepper
- 2 tablespoons harissa paste
- 6 ounces Greek yogurt
- Juice of 1 lemon
- ¼ cup red onion, chopped
- ¼ cup parsley, chopped

Directions:
1. Put the potatoes in a pot, add water to cover, add salt, bring to a boil over medium-high heat, cook for 12 minutes, drain and transfer them to a bowl.
2. Add the harissa and the rest of the ingredients, toss and serve for lunch.

Nutrition Info:
- calories 354, fat 19.2, fiber 4.5, carbs 24.7, protein 11.2

Creamy Chicken Soup

Servings: 8
Cooking Time: 1 Hour

Ingredients:
- 2 cups eggplant, cubed
- Salt and black pepper to the taste
- ¼ cup olive oil
- 1 yellow onion, chopped
- 2 tablespoons garlic, minced
- 1 red bell pepper, chopped
- 2 tablespoons hot paprika
- ¼ cup parsley, chopped
- 1 and ½ tablespoons oregano, chopped
- 4 cups chicken stock
- 1 pound chicken breast, skinless, boneless and cubed
- 1 cup half and half
- 2 egg yolks
- ¼ cup lime juice

Directions:
1. Heat up a pot with the oil over medium heat, add the chicken, garlic and onion, and brown for 10 minutes.
2. Add the bell pepper and the rest of the ingredients except the half and half, egg, yolks and the lime juice, bring to a simmer and cook over medium heat for 40 minutes.
3. In a bowl, combine the egg yolks with the remaining ingredients with 1 cup of soup, whisk well and pour into the pot.
4. Whisk the soup, cook for 5 minutes more, divide into bowls and serve.

Nutrition Info:
- calories 312, fat 17.4, fiber 5.6, carbs 20.2, protein 15.3

Tomato Roasted Feta

Servings: 4
Cooking Time:45 Minutes

Ingredients:
- 8 oz. feta cheese
- 2 tomatoes, peeled and diced
- 2 garlic cloves, chopped
- 1 cup tomato juice
- 1 thyme sprig
- 1 oregano sprig

Directions:
1. Mix the tomatoes, garlic, tomato juice, thyme and oregano in a small deep dish baking pan.
2. Place the feta in the pan as well and cover with aluminum foil.
3. Cook in the preheated oven at 350F for 10 minutes.
4. Serve the feta and the sauce fresh.

Nutrition Info:
- Per Serving:Calories:173 Fat:12.2g Protein:9.2g Carbohydrates:7.8g

Sausage Ragout

Servings: 10
Cooking Time:1 ¼ Hours

Ingredients:
- 3 tablespoons olive oil
- 1 pound beef sausages
- 2 pounds pork sausages
- 3 sweet onions, chopped
- 4 garlic cloves, minced
- 2 carrots, grated
- 2 celery stalks, chopped
- 2 red bell peppers, cored and diced
- 1 jalapeno, chopped
- 1 teaspoon ground coriander
- 1 teaspoon cumin powder
- 1 teaspoon smoked paprika
- 1 can chickpeas, drained
- 1 can diced tomatoes
- 1 ½ cups chicken stock
- ¼ cup white wine
- Salt and pepper to taste
- 1 bay leaf
- 1 thyme sprig

Directions:
1. Remove the casings off the sausages and shred the meat.
2. Heat the oil in a skillet or deep heavy saucepan and stir in the sausages.
3. Cook for 10 minutes then add the onions and garlic and cook for another 5 minutes.
4. Stir in the rest of the ingredients and season with salt and pepper.
5. Cover the pot with a lid and cook on low heat for 1 hour.
6. Serve the ragout warm.

Nutrition Info:
- Per Serving:Calories:405 Fat:33.8g Protein:16.0g Carbohydrates:7.9g

Mediterranean Tarts

Servings: 2
Cooking Time:40 Minutes

Ingredients:
- 1 tablespoon pesto
- 1 teaspoon sugar, light muscovado
- 100 g Camembert cheese, cut into slices
- 100 g green bean, lightly steamed
- 2 large onion, thinly sliced
- 2 tablespoons olive oil, plus more
- 200 g cherry tomato on the vine, sliced into halves, reserve 2 sprigs with 3-4 tomatoes on each stem
- 250 g ready-made whole-wheat puff pastry, thawed if frozen
- 50 g rocket leaves (arugula), preferably wild
- 6 anchovy fillets, optional
- 6 black olive, not pitted
- 6 medium new potato
- A few basil leaves, roughly torn
- Good squeeze of lemon juice
- Knob butter

Directions:
1. Heat the butter with 1 tablespoon olive oil until the butter is melted. Add the onions; cook over medium-low heat for about 15-20 minutes, stirring often, until the onions are golden brown and soft.
2. Add the sugar, stirring, and cook for 3 to 4 minutes more; remove from heat and let cool.
3. Cook the potatoes in boiling salted water for about 10 minutes or until just tender; let cool enough to handle then slice.
4. Preheat the oven to 220C, gas to 7, or fan to 200C.
5. Divide the pastry into two; shape into rough rounds. On a lightly floured surface, roll each dough into 18-cm or 7-in rounds; place into baking sheet.
6. Divide the caramelized onions between the two rounds, spreading to cove r the surface.
7. Sprinkle the cheese over the onions. Top with the sliced potatoes, the sliced tomatoes, and if using, the anchovy fillets. Top with the reserved tomatoes on the vine. Scatter with the olives and drizzle with a bit of olive oil; bake for about 15 to 20 minutes, or until golden.
8. Mix the pesto with the remaining 1 tablespoon of olive oil. Toss the beans and the rocket leaves with a little olive oil and the lemon juice; season.
9. When the tarts are baked, drizzle the top with the pesto mixture.
10. Serve with the green bean and rocket salad.

Nutrition Info:
- Per Serving:1025Cal, 63 g total fat (13 g sat. fat), 93 g carb.,3 g sugar, 7 g fiber, 28 g protein, and 3.49 g sodium.

Greek Beef Meatballs

Servings: 8
Cooking Time:1 Hour

Ingredients:
- 2 pounds ground beef
- 6 garlic cloves, minced
- 1 teaspoon dried mint
- 1 teaspoon dried oregano
- 1 shallot, finely chopped
- 1 carrot, grated
- 1 egg
- 1 tablespoon tomato paste
- 3 tablespoons chopped parsley
- Salt and pepper to taste

Directions:
1. Combine all the ingredients in a bowl and mix well.
2. Season with salt and pepper then form small meatballs and place them in a baking tray lined with baking paper.
3. Bake in the preheated oven at 350F for 25 minutes.
4. Serve the meatballs warm and fresh.

Nutrition Info:
- Per Serving:Calories:229 Fat:7.7g Protein:35.5g Carbohydrates:2.4g

Poultry Recipes

Chicken And Ginger Cucumbers Mix

Servings: 4
Cooking Time: 20 Minutes

Ingredients:

- 4 chicken breasts, boneless, skinless and cubed
- 2 cucumbers, cubed
- Salt and black pepper to the taste
- 1 tablespoon ginger, grated
- 1 tablespoon garlic, minced
- 2 tablespoons balsamic vinegar
- 3 tablespoons olive oil
- ¼ teaspoon chili paste
- ½ cup chicken stock
- ½ tablespoon lime juice
- 1 tablespoon chives, chopped

Directions:

1. Heat up a pan with the oil over medium-high heat, add the chicken and brown for 3 minutes on each side.
2. Add the cucumbers, salt, pepper and the rest of the ingredients except the chives, bring to a simmer and cook over medium heat for 15 minutes.
3. Divide the mix between plates and serve with the chives sprinkled on top.

Nutrition Info:

- calories 288, fat 9.5, fiber 12.1, carbs 25.6, protein 28.6

Herbed Almond Turkey

Servings: 4
Cooking Time: 40 Minutes

Ingredients:

- 1 big turkey breast, skinless, boneless and cubed
- 1 tablespoon olive oil
- ½ cup chicken stock
- 1 tablespoon basil, chopped
- 1 tablespoon rosemary, chopped
- 1 tablespoon oregano, chopped
- 1 tablespoon parsley, chopped
- 3 garlic cloves, minced
- ½ cup almonds, toasted and chopped
- 3 cups tomatoes, chopped

Directions:

1. Heat up a pan with the oil over medium-high heat, add the turkey and the garlic and brown for 5 minutes.
2. Add the stock and the rest of the ingredients, bring to a simmer over medium heat and cook for 35 minutes.
3. Divide the mix between plates and serve.

Nutrition Info:

- calories 297, fat 11.2, fiber 9.2, carbs 19.4, protein 23.6

Ginger Chicken Drumsticks

Servings:4
Cooking Time: 30 Minutes

Ingredients:

- 4 chicken drumsticks
- 1 apple, grated
- 1 tablespoon curry paste
- 4 tablespoons milk
- 1 teaspoon coconut oil
- 1 teaspoon chili flakes
- ½ teaspoon minced ginger

Directions:

1. Mix up together grated apple, curry paste, milk, chili flakes, and minced garlic.
2. Put coconut oil in the skillet and melt it.
3. Add apple mixture and stir well.
4. Then add chicken drumsticks and mix up well.
5. Roast the chicken for 2 minutes from each side.
6. Then preheat oven to 360F.
7. Place the skillet with chicken drumsticks in the oven and bake for 25 minutes.

Nutrition Info:

- Per Servingcalories 150, fat 6.4, fiber 1.4, carbs 9.7, protein 13.5

Chicken And Lemongrass Sauce

Servings:4
Cooking Time: 20 Minutes

Ingredients:

- 1 tablespoon dried dill
- 1 teaspoon butter, melted
- ½ teaspoon lemongrass
- ½ teaspoon cayenne pepper
- 1 teaspoon tomato sauce
- 3 tablespoons sour cream
- 1 teaspoon salt
- 10 oz chicken fillet, cubed

Directions:

1. Make the sauce: in the saucepan whisk together lemongrass, tomato sauce, sour cream, salt, and dried dill.
2. Bring the sauce to boil.
3. Meanwhile, pour melted butter in the skillet.
4. Add cubed chicken fillet and roast it for 5 minutes. Stir it from time to time.

5. Then place the chicken cubes in the hot sauce.

6. Close the lid and cook the meal for 10 minutes over the low heat.

Nutrition Info:

• Per Servingcalories 166, fat 8.2, fiber 0.2, carbs 1.1, protein 21

Creamy Chicken

Servings:4

Cooking Time: 35 Minutes

Ingredients:

• 1-pound chicken breast, skinless, boneless
• 3 oz Mozzarella, sliced
• 1 tomato, sliced
• 1 teaspoon Italian seasoning
• ½ teaspoon salt
• 1 tablespoon sour cream
• 1 teaspoon olive oil

Directions:

1. Make the cuts in the chicken breast in the shape of Hasselback.

2. Sprinkle the chicken with Italian seasoning, salt, and sour cream.

3. Massage the chicken breast gently.

4. Fill every chicken breast cut with sliced Mozzarella and sliced tomato.

5. Arrange the chicken breast in the baking dish and sprinkle it with olive oil.

6. Bake the chicken Hasselback for 35 minutes at 355F.

Nutrition Info:

• Per Servingcalories 212, fat 8.8, fiber 0.2, carbs 1.6, protein 30.3

Chicken With Artichokes And Beans

Servings: 4

Cooking Time: 40 Minutes

Ingredients:

• 2 tablespoons olive oil
• 2 chicken breasts, skinless, boneless and halved
• Zest of 1 lemon, grated
• 3 garlic cloves, crushed
• Juice of 1 lemon
• Salt and black pepper to the taste
• 1 tablespoon thyme, chopped
• 6 ounces canned artichokes hearts, drained
• 1 cup canned fava beans, drained and rinsed
• 1 cup chicken stock
• A pinch of cayenne pepper
• Salt and black pepper to the taste

Directions:

1. Heat up a pan with the oil over medium-high heat, add chicken and brown for 5 minutes.

2. Add lemon juice, lemon zest, salt, pepper and the rest of the ingredients, bring to a simmer and cook over medium heat for 35 minutes.

3. Divide the mix between plates and serve right away.

Nutrition Info:

• calories 291, fat 14.9, fiber 10.5, carbs 23.8, protein 24.2

Parmesan Chicken And Pineapple

Servings:4

Cooking Time: 30 Minutes

Ingredients:

• 2 chicken thighs, skinless, boneless
• 1 teaspoon paprika
• 1 tablespoon lemon juice
• ½ teaspoon chili flakes
• ¼ teaspoon garlic powder
• 3 oz Parmesan, grated
• 1/3 cup milk
• 1 onion, sliced
• 2 oz pineapple, sliced

Directions:

1. Chop the chicken thighs roughly and sprinkle them with paprika, lemon juice, chili flakes, garlic powder, and mix up well.

2. Arrange the chopped chicken thighs in the baking dish in one layer.

3. Then place sliced onion over the chicken.

4. Add the layer of sliced pineapple.

5. Mix up together milk and Parmesan and pour the liquid over the pineapple,

6. Cover the surface of the baking dish with foil and bake gratin for 30 minutes at 355F.

Nutrition Info:

• Per Servingcalories 100, fat 5.2, fiber 1, carbs 6.7, protein 8.1

Chicken And Tzaziki Pitas

Servings:8

Cooking Time: 0 Minutes

Ingredients:

• 4 pita bread
• 10 oz chicken fillet, grilled
• 1 cup lettuce, chopped
• 8 teaspoons tzaziki sauce

Directions:

1. Cut every pita bread on the halves to get 8 pita pockets.

2. Then fill every pita pocket with chopped lettuce and sprinkle greens with tzaziki sauce.

3. Chop chicken fillet and add it in the pita pockets too.

Nutrition Info:

• Per Servingcalories 106, fat 3.8, fiber 0.2, carbs 6.1, protein 11

Chicken With Spinach

Servings:6
Cooking Time: 25 Minutes

Ingredients:
• 14 oz chicken fillet
• 1 tablespoon butter
• ½ teaspoon ground black pepper
• 1 teaspoon salt
• ½ cup cream
• 2 oz Parmesan, grated
• 1 oz sun-dried tomatoes, chopped
• 1 cup fresh spinach, chopped
• ½ teaspoon chili flakes

Directions:
1. Cut the chicken fillet on 6 pieces and sprinkle them with salt and ground black pepper.
2. Toss the butter in the skillet and melt it.
3. Add the chicken fillet pieces and roast them for 5 minutes from each side.
4. After this, remove the chicken fillets from the skillet.
5. Pour cream in the skillet.
6. Add Parmesan, sun-dried tomatoes, spinach, and chili flakes.
7. Bring the mixture to boil and stir well.
8. Add chicken fillets and mix up.
9. Close the lid and cook the meal for 10 minutes over the low heat.

Nutrition Info:
• Per Servingcalories 188, fat 10, fiber 0.2, carbs 1.5, protein 22.6

Lemon Chicken Mix

Servings:2
Cooking Time: 10 Minutes

Ingredients:
• 8 oz chicken breast, skinless, boneless
• 1 teaspoon Cajun seasoning
• 1 teaspoon balsamic vinegar
• 1 teaspoon olive oil
• 1 teaspoon lemon juice

Directions:
1. Cut the chicken breast on the halves and sprinkle with Cajun seasoning.
2. Then sprinkle the poultry with olive oil and lemon juice.
3. Then sprinkle the chicken breast with the balsamic vinegar.
4. Preheat the grill to 385F.
5. Grill the chicken breast halves for 5 minutes from each side.

6. Slice Cajun chicken and place in the serving plate.

Nutrition Info:
• Per Servingcalories 150, fat 5.2, fiber 0, carbs 0.1, protein 24.1

Cardamom Chicken And Apricot Sauce

Servings: 4
Cooking Time: 7 Hours

Ingredients:
• Juice of ½ lemon
• Zest of ½ lemon, grated
• 2 teaspoons cardamom, ground
• Salt and black pepper to the taste
• 2 chicken breasts, skinless, boneless and halved
• 2 tablespoons olive oil
• 2 spring onions, chopped
• 2 tablespoons tomato paste
• 2 garlic cloves, minced
• 1 cup apricot juice
• ½ cup chicken stock
• ¼ cup cilantro, chopped

Directions:
1. In your slow cooker, combine the chicken with the lemon juice, lemon zest and the other ingredients except the cilantro, toss, put the lid on and cook on Low for 7 hours.
2. Divide the mix between plates, sprinkle the cilantro on top and serve.

Nutrition Info:
• calories 323, fat 12, fiber 11, carbs 23.8, protein 16.4

Chicken And Olives Salsa

Servings: 4
Cooking Time: 25 Minutes

Ingredients:
• 2 tablespoon avocado oil
• 4 chicken breast halves, skinless and boneless
• Salt and black pepper to the taste
• 1 tablespoon sweet paprika
• 1 red onion, chopped
• 1 tablespoon balsamic vinegar
• 2 tablespoons parsley, chopped
• 1 avocado, peeled, pitted and cubed
• 2 tablespoons black olives, pitted and chopped

Directions:
1. Heat up your grill over medium-high heat, add the chicken brushed with half of the oil and seasoned with paprika, salt and pepper, cook for 7 minutes on each side and divide between plates.
2. Meanwhile, in a bowl, mix the onion with the rest of the ingredients and the remaining oil, toss, add on top of the chicken and serve.

Nutrition Info:
- calories 289, fat 12.4, fiber 9.1, carbs 23.8, protein 14.3

Honey Chicken

Servings:5
Cooking Time: 25 Minutes

Ingredients:
- 5 chicken drumsticks
- 2 oz currant
- ½ teaspoon liquid honey
- 1 teaspoon butter
- 1 teaspoon lime juice
- ½ teaspoon salt
- ¼ cup of water
- ½ teaspoon chili pepper

Directions:
1. Mix up together chicken drumsticks with chili pepper and salt.
2. Put butter in the skillet and heat it up.
3. Add chicken drumsticks and cook them for 15 minutes or until they are cooked.
4. Meanwhile, mash currant and mix it up with lime juice, liquid honey, and water.
5. Pour the currant mixture over the drumstick and close the lid.
6. Cook the meal for 5 minutes over the medium heat.

Nutrition Info:
- Per Servingcalories 93, fat 3.4, fiber 0.5, carbs 2.2, protein 12.8

Chicken With Artichokes

Servings:3
Cooking Time: 30 Minutes

Ingredients:
- 1 can artichoke hearts, chopped
- 12 oz chicken fillets (3 oz each fillet)
- 1 teaspoon avocado oil
- ½ teaspoon ground thyme
- ½ teaspoon white pepper
- 1/3 cup water
- 1/3 cup shallot, roughly chopped
- 1 lemon, sliced

Directions:
1. Mix up together chicken fillets, artichoke hearts, avocado oil, ground thyme, white pepper, and shallot.
2. Line the baking tray with baking paper and place the chicken fillet mixture in it.
3. Then add sliced lemon and water.
4. Bake the meal for 30 minutes at 375F. Stir the ingredients during cooking to avoid burning.

Nutrition Info:

- Per Servingcalories 263, fat 8.8, fiber 3.7, carbs 10.9, protein 35.3

Slow Cooked Chicken And Capers Mix

Servings: 4
Cooking Time: 7 Hours

Ingredients:
- 2 chicken breasts, skinless, boneless and halved
- 2 cups canned tomatoes, crushed
- 2 garlic cloves, minced
- 1 yellow onion, chopped
- 2 cups chicken stock
- 2 tablespoons capers, drained
- ¼ cup rosemary, chopped
- Salt and black pepper to the taste

Directions:
1. In your slow cooker, combine the chicken with the tomatoes, capers and the rest of the ingredients, put the lid on and cook on Low for 7 hours.
2. Divide the mix between plates and serve.

Nutrition Info:
- calories 292, fat 9.4, fiber 11.8, carbs 25.1, protein 36.4

Orange Duck And Celery

Servings: 4
Cooking Time: 40 Minutes

Ingredients:
- 2 duck legs, boneless, skinless
- 1 tablespoon avocado oil
- 1 cup chicken stock
- Salt and black pepper to the taste
- 4 celery ribs, roughly chopped
- 2 garlic cloves, minced
- 1 red onion, chopped
- 2 teaspoons thyme, dried
- 2 tablespoons tomato paste
- Zest of 1 orange, grated
- Juice of 2 oranges
- 3 oranges, peeled and cut into segments

Directions:
1. Grease a roasting pan with the oil, add the duck legs, the stock, salt, pepper and the other ingredients, toss a bit and bake at 450 degrees F for 40 minutes.
2. Divide everything between plates and serve warm.

Nutrition Info:
- calories 294, fat 12.4, fiber 11.3, carbs 25.5, protein 16.4

Turkey And Salsa Verde

Servings: 4
Cooking Time: 50 Minutes

Ingredients:

- 1 big turkey breast, skinless, boneless and cubed
- 1 and ½ cups Salsa Verde
- Salt and black pepper to the taste
- 1 tablespoon olive oil
- 1 and ½ cups feta cheese, crumbled
- ¼ cup cilantro, chopped

Directions:

1. In a roasting pan greased with the oil combine the turkey with the salsa, salt and pepper and bake 400 degrees F for 50 minutes.
2. Add the cheese and the cilantro, toss gently, divide everything between plates and serve.

Nutrition Info:

- calories 332, fat 15.4, fiber 10.5, carbs 22.1, protein 34.5

Dill Chicken Stew

Servings:2
Cooking Time: 25 Minutes

Ingredients:

- 1 ½ cup water
- 6 oz chicken fillet
- 1 chili pepper, chopped
- 1 onion, diced
- 1 teaspoon butter
- ½ teaspoon salt
- ½ teaspoon paprika
- 1 tablespoon fresh dill, chopped

Directions:

1. Pour water in the saucepan.
2. Add chicken fillet and salt. Boil it for 15 minutes over the medium heat.
3. Then remove the chicken fillet from water and shred it with the help of the fork.
4. Return it back in the hot water.
5. Melt butter in the skillet and add diced onion. Roast it until light brown and transfer in the shredded chicken.
6. Add paprika, dill, chili pepper, and mix up.
7. Close the lid and simmer Posole for 5 minutes.
8. Ladle it in the serving bowls.

Nutrition Info:

- Per Servingcalories 207, fat 8.4, fiber 1.7, carbs 6.5, protein 25.7

Chicken With Peas

Servings:4
Cooking Time: 30 Minutes

Ingredients:

- 4 chicken fillets
- 1 teaspoon cayenne pepper
- 1 teaspoon salt
- 1 tablespoon mayonnaise
- 1 cup green peas
- ¼ cup of water
- 1 carrot, peeled, chopped

Directions:

1. Sprinkle the chicken fillet with cayenne pepper and salt.
2. Line the baking tray with foil and place chicken fillets in it.
3. Then brush the chicken with mayonnaise.
4. Add carrot and green peas.
5. Then add water and cover the ingredients with foil.
6. Bake the chicken for 30 minutes at 355F.

Nutrition Info:

- Per Servingcalories 329 fat 12.3, fiber 2.3, carbs 7.9, protein 44.4

Ginger Duck Mix

Servings: 4
Cooking Time: 1 Hour And 50 Minutes

Ingredients:

- 4 duck legs, boneless
- 4 shallots, chopped
- 2 tablespoons olive oil
- 1 tablespoon ginger, grated
- 2 tablespoons rosemary, chopped
- 1 cup chicken stock
- 1 tablespoon chives, chopped

Directions:

1. In a roasting pan, combine the duck legs with the shallots and the rest of the ingredients except the chives, toss, introduce in the oven at 250 degrees F and bake for 1 hour and 30 minutes.
2. Divide the mix between plates, sprinkle the chives on top and serve.

Nutrition Info:

- calories 299, fat 10.2, fiber 9.2, carbs 18.1, protein 17.3

Saffron Chicken Thighs And Green Beans

Servings: 4
Cooking Time: 25 Minutes

Ingredients:
- 2 pounds chicken thighs, boneless and skinless
- 2 teaspoons saffron powder
- 1 pound green beans, trimmed and halved
- ½ cup Greek yogurt
- Salt and black pepper to the taste
- 1 tablespoon lime juice
- 1 tablespoon dill, chopped

Directions:
1. In a roasting pan, combine the chicken with the saffron, green beans and the rest of the ingredients, toss a bit, introduce in the oven and bake at 400 degrees F for 25 minutes.
2. Divide everything between plates and serve.

Nutrition Info:
- calories 274, fat 12.3, fiber 5.3, carbs 20.4, protein 14.3

Lime Turkey And Avocado Mix

Servings: 2
Cooking Time: 1 Hour And 10 Minutes

Ingredients:
- 2 tablespoons olive oil
- 1 turkey breast, boneless, skinless and halved
- 2 ounces cherry tomatoes, halved
- A handful coriander, chopped
- Juice of 1 lime
- Zest of 1 lime, grated
- Salt and black pepper to the taste
- 2 spring onions, chopped
- 2 avocadoes, pitted, peeled and cubed

Directions:
1. In a roasting pan, combine the turkey with the oil and the rest of the ingredients, introduce in the oven and bake at 370 degrees F for 1 hour and 10 minutes.
2. Divide between plates and serve.

Nutrition Info:
- calories 301, fat 8.9, fiber 10.2, carbs 19.8, protein 13.5

Chicken And Veggie Saute

Servings:2
Cooking Time: 25 Minutes

Ingredients:
- 4 oz chicken fillet
- 4 tomatoes, peeled
- 1 bell pepper, chopped
- 1 teaspoon olive oil
- 1 cup of water
- 1 teaspoon salt
- 1 chili pepper, chopped
- ½ teaspoon saffron

Directions:
1. Pour water in the pan and bring it to boil.
2. Meanwhile, chop the chicken fillet.
3. Add the chicken fillet in the boiling water and cook it for 10 minutes or until the chicken is tender.
4. After this, put the chopped bell pepper and chili pepper in the skillet.
5. Add olive oil and roast the vegetables for 3 minutes.
6. Add chopped tomatoes and mix up well.
7. Cook the vegetables for 2 minutes more.
8. Then add salt and a ¾ cup of water from chicken.
9. Add chopped chicken fillet and mix up.
10. Cook the saute for 10 minutes over the medium heat.

Nutrition Info:
- Per Servingcalories 192, fat 7.2, fiber 3.8, carbs 14.4, protein 19.2

Fish And Seafood Recipes

Rosemary Salmon

Servings:5
Cooking Time: 10 Minutes

Ingredients:
- 2-pound salmon fillet
- 2 tablespoons avocado oil
- 2 teaspoons fresh rosemary, chopped
- ½ teaspoon minced garlic
- ½ teaspoon dried cilantro
- ½ teaspoon salt
- 1 teaspoon butter
- ½ teaspoon white pepper

Directions:
1. Whisk together avocado oil, fresh rosemary, minced garlic, dried cilantro, salt, and white pepper.
2. Rub the salmon fillet with the rosemary mixture generously and leave fish in the fridge for 20 minutes to marinate.
3. After this, put butter in the saucepan or big skillet and melt it.
4. Then put heat on maximum and place a salmon fillet in the hot butter.
5. Roast it for 1 minute from each side.
6. After this, preheat grill to 385F and grill the fillet for 8 minutes (for 4 minutes from each side).
7. Cut the cooked salmon on the servings.

Nutrition Info:
- Per Servingcalories 257, fat 12.8, fiber 0.5, carbs 0.9, protein 35.3

Trout And Tzatziki Sauce

Servings: 4
Cooking Time: 10 Minutes

Ingredients:
- Juice of ½ lime
- Salt and black pepper to the taste
- 1 and ½ teaspoon coriander, ground
- 1 teaspoon garlic, minced
- 4 trout fillets, boneless
- 1 teaspoon sweet paprika
- 2 tablespoons avocado oil
- For the sauce:
- 1 cucumber, chopped
- 4 garlic cloves, minced
- 1 tablespoon olive oil
- 1 teaspoon white vinegar
- 1 and ½ cups Greek yogurt

- A pinch of salt and white pepper

Directions:
1. Heat up a pan with the avocado oil over medium-high heat, add the fish, salt, pepper, lime juice, 1 teaspoon garlic and the paprika, rub the fish gently and cook for 4 minutes on each side.
2. In a bowl, combine the cucumber with 4 garlic cloves and the rest of the ingredients for the sauce and whisk well.
3. Divide the fish between plates, drizzle the sauce all over and serve with a side salad.

Nutrition Info:
- calories 393, fat 18.5, fiber 6.5, carbs 18.3, protein 39.6

Halibut And Tomatoes

Servings:5
Cooking Time: 30 Minutes

Ingredients:
- 1-pound halibut, chopped
- 1 teaspoon chili pepper
- 1 teaspoon paprika
- 1 teaspoon minced garlic
- ½ teaspoon dried oregano
- ¼ teaspoon dried parsley
- ½ cup tomatoes, chopped
- 1/3 cup water
- 1 teaspoon salt
- 1 teaspoon olive oil
- 1 yellow onion, chopped

Directions:
1. Pour olive oil in the saucepan and preheat it.
2. Add chopped onion and roast it for 5 minutes over the medium heat. Stir the vegetables from time to time.
3. Then add salt, tomatoes, and minced garlic. Mix up the ingredients well with the help of the spatula.
4. Cook the vegetables until tomatoes start to give juice.
5. Then add chopped halibut.
6. Sprinkle the mixture with chili pepper, paprika, dried oregano, dried parsley, and mix up well.
7. Then add water and bring the fish to boil.
8. Close the lid and cook the fish for 15 minutes over the medium heat.

Nutrition Info:
- Per Servingcalories 144, fat 3.3, fiber 1, carbs 3.4, protein 25.8

Fish And Rice (sayadieh)

Serves: 1 Cup
Cooking Time:1½hours

Ingredients:

- 1 lb. whitefish fillets (cod, tilapia, or haddock)
- 2 tsp. salt
- 2 tsp. ground black pepper
- 1/4 cup plus 2 TB. extra-virgin olive oil
- 2 large yellow onions, sliced
- 5 cups water
- 1 tsp. turmeric
- 1 tsp. ground coriander
- 1/2 tsp. ground cumin
- 1/4 tsp. ground cinnamon
- 2 cups basmati rice
- 1/2 cup sliced almonds

Directions:

1. Season both sides of whitefish with 1 teaspoon salt and 1 teaspoon black pepper.
2. In a skillet over medium heat, heat 1/4 cup extra-virgin olive oil. Add fish, and cook for 3 minutes per side. Remove fish from the pan.
3. Add yellow onions to the skillet, reduce heat to medium-low, and cook for 15 minutes or until golden brown and caramelized.
4. In a 3-quart pot over medium heat, add 1/2 of cooked onions, water, turmeric, coriander, cumin, cinnamon, remaining 1 teaspoon salt, and remaining 1 teaspoon black pepper. Simmer for 20 minutes.
5. Add basmati rice, cover, and cook for 30 minutes.
6. Cut fish into 1/2-inch pieces, fluff rice, and gently fold fish into rice. Cover and cook for 10 more minutes.
7. Remove from heat, and let sit for 10 minutes before serving.
8. Meanwhile, in a small saucepan over low heat, heat remaining 2 tablespoons extra-virgin olive oil. Add almonds, and toast for 3 minutes.
9. Spoon fish and rice onto a serving plate, top with remaining onions and toasted almonds, and serve.

Italian Tuna Pasta

Servings: 6
Cooking Time: 5 Minutes

Ingredients:

- 15 oz whole wheat pasta
- 2 tbsp capers
- 3 oz tuna
- 2 cups can tomatoes, crushed
- 2 anchovies
- 1 tsp garlic, minced
- 1 tbsp olive oil
- Salt

Directions:

1. Add oil into the inner pot of instant pot and set the pot on sauté mode.
2. Add anchovies and garlic and sauté for 1 minute.
3. Add remaining ingredients and stir well. Pour enough water into the pot to cover the pasta.
4. Seal pot with a lid and select manual and cook on low for 4 minutes.
5. Once done, release pressure using quick release. Remove lid.
6. Stir and serve.

Nutrition Info:

- Calories 339 Fat 6 g Carbohydrates 56.5 g Sugar 5.2 g Protein 15.2 g Cholesterol 10 mg

Seafood And Potato Bake

Servings:5
Cooking Time: 40 Minutes

Ingredients:

- 3 Russet potatoes, sliced
- ½ cup onion, chopped
- ½ cup milk
- 1 egg, beaten
- 3 tablespoon wheat flour, whole grain
- 1 cup shrimps, peeled
- ½ cup Mozzarella cheese, shredded
- ¼ cup Cheddar cheese, shredded
- 1 teaspoon olive oil
- 1 cup water, for cooking

Directions:

1. Pour water in the pan and bring it to boil.
2. Add sliced potatoes in the hot water and boil it for 3 minutes.
3. Then remove potatoes from water.
4. Mix up together beaten egg, milk, chopped onion, flour, and Cheddar cheese.
5. Preheat the mixture until cheese is melted.
6. Then place the potatoes in the gratin mold in one layer.
7. Add the layer of shrimps.
8. Pour Cheddar cheese mixture over shrimps and top the gratin with Mozzarella cheese.
9. Cover the gratin with foil and secure the edges.
10. Bake gratin for 35 minutes at 355F.

Nutrition Info:

- Per Servingcalories 205, fat 5.3, fiber 3.5, carbs 26.2, protein 14.1

Roasted Halibut With Banana Relish

Servings: 4
Cooking Time: 12 Minutes

Ingredients:
- ¼ cup cilantro
- ½ tsp freshly grated orange zest
- ½ tsp kosher salt, divided
- 1 lb. halibut or any deep-water fish
- 1 tsp ground coriander, divided into half
- 2 oranges (peeled, segmented and chopped)
- 2 ripe bananas, diced
- 2 tbsp lime juice

Directions:
1. In a pan, prepare the fish by rubbing ½ tsp coriander and ¼ tsp kosher salt.
2. Place in a baking sheet with cooking spray and bake for 8 to 12 minutes inside a 450-degree Fahrenheit preheated oven.
3. Prepare the relish by stirring the orange zest, bananas, chopped oranges, lime juice, cilantro and the rest of the salt and coriander in a medium bowl.
4. Spoon the relish over the roasted fish.
5. Serve and enjoy.

Nutrition Info:
- Calories per serving: 245.7; Protein: 15.3g; Fat: 6g; Carbs: 21g

Pepper Salmon Skewers

Servings:5
Cooking Time: 15 Minutes

Ingredients:
- 1.5-pound salmon fillet
- ½ cup Plain yogurt
- 1 teaspoon paprika
- 1 teaspoon turmeric
- 1 teaspoon red pepper
- 1 teaspoon salt
- 1 teaspoon dried cilantro
- 1 teaspoon sunflower oil
- ½ teaspoon ground nutmeg

Directions:
1. For the marinade: mix up together Plain yogurt, paprika, turmeric red pepper, salt, and ground nutmeg.
2. Chop the salmon fillet roughly and put it in the yogurt mixture.
3. Mix up well and marinate for 25 minutes.
4. Then skew the fish on the skewers.
5. Sprinkle the skewers with sunflower oil and place in the tray.
6. Bake the salmon skewers for 15 minutes at 375F.

Nutrition Info:

- Per Servingcalories 217, fat 9.9, fiber 0.6, carbs 4.2, protein 28.1

Orange Herbed Sauced White Bass

Servings: 6
Cooking Time: 33 Minutes

Ingredients:
- ¼ cup thinly sliced green onions
- ½ cup orange juice
- 1 ½ tbsp fresh lemon juice
- 1 ½ tbsp olive oil
- 1 large onion, halved, thinly sliced
- 1 large orange, unpeeled, sliced
- 3 tbsp chopped fresh dill
- 6 3-oz skinless white bass fillets
- Additional unpeeled orange slices

Directions:
1. Grease a 13 x 9-inch glass baking dish and preheat oven to 400oF.
2. Arrange orange slices in single layer on baking dish, top with onion slices, seasoned with pepper and salt plus drizzled with oil.
3. Pop in the oven and roast for 25 minutes or until onions are tender and browned.
4. Remove from oven and increased oven temperature to 450oF.
5. Push onion and orange slices on sides of dish and place bass fillets in middle of dish. Season with 1 ½ tbsp dill, pepper and salt. Arrange onions and orange slices on top of fish and pop into the oven.
6. Roast for 8 minutes or until salmon is opaque and flaky.
7. In a small bowl, mix 1 ½ tbsp dill, lemon juice, green onions and orange juice.
8. Transfer salmon to a serving plate, discard roasted onions, drizzle with the newly made orange sauce and garnish with fresh orange slices.
9. Serve and enjoy.

Nutrition Info:
- Calories per serving: 312.42; Protein: 84.22; Fat: 23.14; Carbs: 33.91g

Oregano Swordfish Mix

Servings:4
Cooking Time: 20 Minutes

Ingredients:
- 4 swordfish fillets (oz each fillet)
- 4 sprig fresh rosemary
- 4 teaspoons capers
- ½ teaspoon dried oregano
- 1 tablespoon olive oil
- ½ teaspoon salt
- 1 teaspoon butter
- 1 tablespoon lemon juice
- ¼ teaspoon lemon zest, grated

Directions:
1. Toss butter in the skillet and bring it to boil.
2. Add rosemary sprigs, lemon zest, and dried oregano.
3. Boil the ingredients for 20 seconds.
4. Then add swordfish fillets.
5. Roast the fish for 2 minutes from each side over the high heat.
6. Then reduce the heat to medium.
7. Sprinkle the fish with olive oil, salt, lemon juice, and capers.
8. Close the lid and cook the swordfish for 15 minutes over the low heat.

Nutrition Info:
- Per Servingcalories 206, fat 10, fiber 0.3, carbs 0.5, protein 27.1

Cheesy Crab And Lime Spread

Servings: 8
Cooking Time: 25 Minutes

Ingredients:
- 1 pound crab meat, flaked
- 4 ounces cream cheese, soft
- 1 tablespoon chives, chopped
- 1 teaspoon lime juice
- 1 teaspoon lime zest, grated

Directions:
1. In a baking dish greased with cooking spray, combine the crab with the rest of the ingredients and toss.
2. Introduce in the oven at 350 degrees F, bake for 25 minutes, divide into bowls and serve.

Nutrition Info:
- calories 284, fat 14.6, fiber 5.8, carbs 16.5, protein 15.4

Cod And Mushrooms Mix

Servings: 4
Cooking Time: 25 Minutes

Ingredients:
- 2 cod fillets, boneless
- 4 tablespoons olive oil
- 4 ounces mushrooms, sliced
- Sea salt and black pepper to the taste
- 12 cherry tomatoes, halved
- 8 ounces lettuce leaves, torn
- 1 avocado, pitted, peeled and cubed
- 1 red chili pepper, chopped
- 1 tablespoon cilantro, chopped
- 2 tablespoons balsamic vinegar
- 1 ounce feta cheese, crumbled

Directions:
1. Put the fish in a roasting pan, brush it with 2 tablespoons oil, sprinkle salt and pepper all over and broil under medium-high heat for 15 minutes. Meanwhile, heat up a pan with the rest of the oil over medium heat, add the mushrooms, stir and sauté for 5 minutes.
2. Add the rest of the ingredients, toss, cook for 5 minutes more and divide between plates.
3. Top with the fish and serve right away.

Nutrition Info:
- calories 257, fat 10, fiber 3.1, carbs 24.3, protein 19.4

Mahi Mahi And Pomegranate Sauce

Servings: 4
Cooking Time: 10 Minutes

Ingredients:
- 1 and ½ cups chicken stock
- 1 tablespoon olive oil
- 4 mahi mahi fillets, boneless
- 4 tablespoons tahini paste
- Juice of 1 lime
- Seeds from 1 pomegranate
- 1 tablespoon parsley, chopped

Directions:
1. Heat up a pan with the oil over medium-high heat, add the fish and cook for 3 minutes on each side.
2. Add the rest of the ingredients, flip the fish again, cook for 4 minutes more, divide everything between plates and serve.

Nutrition Info:
- calories 224, fat 11.1, fiber 5.5, carbs 16.7, protein 11.4

Orange Halibut

Servings: 4
Cooking Time: 10 Minutes

Ingredients:
- 1-pound halibut
- 1/3 cup butter
- 1 rosemary sprig
- ½ teaspoon ground black pepper
- 1 teaspoon salt
- 1 teaspoon honey
- ¼ cup of orange juice
- 1 teaspoon cornstarch

Directions:
1. Put butter in the saucepan and melt it.
2. Add rosemary sprig.
3. Sprinkle the halibut with salt and ground black pepper.
4. Put the fish in the boiling butter and poach it for 4 minutes.
5. Meanwhile, pour orange juice in the skillet. Add honey and bring the liquid to boil.
6. Add cornstarch and whisk until the liquid will start to be thick.
7. Then remove it from the heat.
8. Transfer the poached halibut in the plate and cut it on 4 servings.
9. Place every fish serving in the serving plate and top with orange sauce.

Nutrition Info:
- Per Servingcalories 349, fat 29.3, fiber 0.1, carbs 3.2, protein 17.8

Garlic Scallops And Peas Mix

Servings: 6
Cooking Time: 20 Minutes

Ingredients:
- 12 ounces scallops
- 2 tablespoons olive oil
- 4 garlic cloves, minced
- A pinch of salt and black pepper
- ½ cup chicken stock
- 1 cup snow peas, sliced
- ½ tablespoon balsamic vinegar
- 1 cup scallions, sliced
- 1 tablespoon basil, chopped

Directions:
1. Heat up a pan with half of the oil over medium-high heat, add the scallops, cook for 5 minutes on each side and transfer to a bowl.
2. Heat up the pan again with the rest of the oil over medium heat, add the scallions and the garlic and sauté for 2 minutes.
3. Add the rest of the ingredients, stir, bring to a simmer and cook for 5 minutes more.
4. Add the scallops to the pan, cook everything for 3 minutes, divide into bowls and serve.

Nutrition Info:
- calories 296, fat 11.8, fiber 9.8, carbs 26.5, protein 20.5

Healthy Halibut Soup

Servings: 4
Cooking Time: 13 Minutes

Ingredients:
- 1 lb halibut, skinless, boneless, & cut into chunks
- 2 tbsp ginger, minced
- 2 celery stalks, chopped
- 1 carrot, sliced
- 1 onion, chopped
- 1 cup of water
- 2 cups fish stock
- 1 tbsp olive oil
- Pepper
- Salt

Directions:
1. Add oil into the inner pot of instant pot and set the pot on sauté mode.
2. Add onion and sauté for 3-4 minutes.
3. Add water, celery, carrot, ginger, and stock and stir well.
4. Seal pot with lid and cook on high for 5 minutes.
5. Once done, release pressure using quick release. Remove lid.
6. Add fish and stir well. Seal pot again and cook on high for 4 minutes.
7. Once done, release pressure using quick release. Remove lid.
8. Stir and serve.

Nutrition Info:
- Calories 4586 Fat 99.6 g Carbohydrates 6.3 g Sugar 2.1 g Protein 861 g Cholesterol 1319 mg

Dill Calamari

Servings:4
Cooking Time: 5 Minutes

Ingredients:
- 1-pound calamari
- 3 tablespoons lime juice
- 1 tablespoon fresh dill, chopped
- 1/3 teaspoon minced garlic
- 1 tablespoon butter
- 1/3 teaspoon salt
- ¼ teaspoon chili pepper

Directions:
1. Slice cleaned and washed calamari into the rings and after this, place them in the mixing bowl.
2. Sprinkle the calamari rings with salt and chili pepper. Mix up well.
3. After this, toss the butter in the skillet and melt it.
4. Add minced garlic, dill, and lime juice.
5. Bring the liquid to boil and add calamari rings.
6. Cook the seafood for 3 minutes over the medium-high heat. Stir them once during the cooking time.
7. Remove the cooked calamari rings from the heat and transfer in the serving plates.

Nutrition Info:
- Per Servingcalories 137, fat 6.9, fiber 0.7, carbs 9.6, protein 8.2

Tarragon Snapper Mix

Servings:3
Cooking Time: 20 Minutes

Ingredients:
- 10 oz snapper fillet
- 1 tablespoon fresh dill, chopped
- 1 white onion, peeled, sliced
- ½ teaspoon tarragon
- 1 tablespoon olive oil
- 1 teaspoon salt
- ½ teaspoon hot pepper
- 2 tablespoons sour cream

Directions:
1. Make the medium size packets from parchment and arrange them in the baking tray.
2. Cut the snapper fillet on 3 servings and sprinkle them with salt, tarragon, and hot pepper.
3. Put the fish fillets in the parchment packets.
4. Then top the fish with olive oil, sour cream sliced onion, and fresh dill.
5. Bake the fish for 20 minutes at 355F.

Nutrition Info:
- Per Servingcalories 204, fat 8.2, fiber 1, carbs 4.6, protein 27.2

Sardine Meatballs

Servings:4
Cooking Time: 10 Minutes

Ingredients:
- 11 oz sardines, canned, drained
- 1/3 cup shallot, chopped
- 1 teaspoon chili flakes
- ½ teaspoon salt
- 2 tablespoon wheat flour, whole grain
- 1 egg, beaten
- 1 tablespoon chives, chopped
- 1 teaspoon olive oil
- 1 teaspoon butter

Directions:
1. Put the butter in the skillet and melt it.
2. Add shallot and cook it until translucent.
3. After this, transfer the shallot in the mixing bowl.
4. Add sardines, chili flakes, salt, flour, egg, chives, and mix up until smooth with the help of the fork.
5. Make the medium size cakes and place them in the skillet.
6. Add olive oil.
7. Roast the fish cakes for 3 minutes from each side over the medium heat.
8. Dry the cooked fish cakes with the paper towel if needed and transfer in the serving plates.

Nutrition Info:
- Per Servingcalories 221, fat 12.2, fiber 0.1, carbs 5.4, protein 21.3

Baked Salmon

Servings:4
Cooking Time: 30 Minutes

Ingredients:
- 4 fresh thyme sprig
- 4 garlic cloves, peeled, roughly chopped
- 16 oz salmon fillets (4 oz each fillet)
- ½ teaspoon salt
- ½ teaspoon ground black pepper
- 4 tablespoons cream
- 4 teaspoons butter
- ¼ teaspoon cumin seeds

Directions:
1. Line the baking tray with foil.
2. Sprinkle the fish fillets with salt, ground black pepper, cumin seeds, and arrange them in the tray with oil.
3. Add thyme sprig on the top of every fillet.
4. Then add cream, butter, and garlic.
5. Bake the fish for 30 minutes at 345F.

Nutrition Info:
- Per Servingcalories 198, fat 11.6, fiber 0.2, carbs 1.8, protein 22.4

Halibut And Quinoa Mix

Servings: 4
Cooking Time: 12 Minutes

Ingredients:
- 4 halibut fillets, boneless
- 2 tablespoons olive oil
- 1 teaspoon rosemary, dried
- 2 teaspoons cumin, ground
- 1 tablespoons coriander, ground
- 2 teaspoons cinnamon powder
- 2 teaspoons oregano, dried
- A pinch of salt and black pepper
- 2 cups quinoa, cooked
- 1 cup cherry tomatoes, halved
- 1 avocado, peeled, pitted and sliced
- 1 cucumber, cubed
- ½ cup black olives, pitted and sliced
- Juice of 1 lemon

Directions:
1. In a bowl, combine the fish with the rosemary, cumin, coriander, cinnamon, oregano, salt and pepper and toss.
2. Heat up a pan with the oil over medium heat, add the fish, and sear for 2 minutes on each side.
3. Introduce the pan in the oven and bake the fish at 425 degrees F for 7 minutes.
4. Meanwhile, in a bowl, mix the quinoa with the remaining ingredients, toss and divide between plates.
5. Add the fish next to the quinoa mix and serve right away.

Nutrition Info:
- calories 364, fat 15.4, fiber 11.2, carbs 56.4, protein 24.5

Pan Fried Tuna With Herbs And Nut

Servings: 4
Cooking Time: 5 Minutes

Ingredients:
- ¼ cup almonds, chopped finely
- ¼ cup fresh tangerine juice
- ½ tsp fennel seeds, chopped finely
- ½ tsp ground pepper, divided
- ½ tsp sea salt, divided
- 1 tbsp olive oil
- 2 tbsp. fresh mint, chopped finely
- 2 tbsp. red onion, chopped finely
- 4 pieces of 6-oz Tuna steak cut in half

Directions:
1. Mix fennel seeds, olive oil, mint, onion, tangerine juice and almonds in small bowl. Season with ¼ each of pepper and salt.
2. Season fish with the remaining pepper and salt.
3. On medium high fire, place a large nonstick fry pan and grease with cooking spray.

4. Pan fry tuna until desired doneness is reached or for one minute per side.
5. Transfer cooked tuna in serving plate, drizzle with dressing and serve.

Nutrition Info:
- Calories per Serving: 272; Fat: 9.7 g; Protein: 42 g; Carbohydrates: 4.2 g

Catfish Steaks

Servings:4
Cooking Time: 10 Minutes

Ingredients:
- 16 oz catfish steaks (4 oz each fish steak)
- 1 tablespoon cajun spices
- 1 egg, beaten
- 1 tablespoon sunflower oil

Directions:
1. Pour sunflower oil in the skillet and preheat it until shimmering.
2. Meanwhile, dip every catfish steak in the beaten egg and coat in Cajun spices.
3. Place the fish steaks in the hot oil and roast them for 4 minutes from each side.
4. The cooked catfish steaks should have a light brown crust.

Nutrition Info:
- Per Servingcalories 263, fat 16.7, fiber 0, carbs 0.1, protein 26.3

Beans & Grains Recipes

Beans & Grains Recipes

Chorizo-kidney Beans Quinoa Pilaf

Servings: 4
Cooking Time: 35 Minutes

Ingredients:
- ¼ pound dried Spanish chorizo diced (about 2/3 cup)
- ¼ teaspoon red pepper flakes
- ¼ teaspoon smoked paprika
- ½ teaspoon cumin
- ½ teaspoon sea salt
- 1 3/4 cups water
- 1 cup quinoa
- 1 large clove garlic minced
- 1 small red bell pepper finely diced
- 1 small red onion finely diced
- 1 tablespoon tomato paste
- 1 15-ounce can kidney beans rinsed and drained

Directions:
1. Place a nonstick pot on medium high fire and heat for 2 minutes. Add chorizo and sauté for 5 minutes until lightly browned.
2. Stir in peppers and onion. Sauté for 5 minutes.
3. Add tomato paste, red pepper flakes, salt, paprika, cumin, and garlic. Sauté for 2 minutes.
4. Stir in quinoa and mix well. Sauté for 2 minutes.
5. Add water and beans. Mix well. Cover and simmer for 20 minutes or until liquid is fully absorbed.
6. Turn off fire and fluff quinoa. Let it sit for 5 minutes more while uncovered.
7. Serve and enjoy.

Nutrition Info:
- Calories per serving: 260; Protein: 9.6g; Carbs: 40.9g; Fat: 6.8g

Pesto Chicken Pasta

Servings: 6
Cooking Time: 10 Minutes

Ingredients:
- 1 lb chicken breast, skinless, boneless, and diced
- 3 tbsp olive oil
- 1/2 cup parmesan cheese, shredded
- 1 tsp Italian seasoning
- 1/4 cup heavy cream
- 16 oz whole wheat pasta
- 6 oz basil pesto
- 3 1/2 cups water
- Pepper
- Salt

Directions:
1. Season chicken with Italian seasoning, pepper, and salt.
2. Add oil into the inner pot of instant pot and set the pot on sauté mode.
3. Add chicken to the pot and sauté until brown.
4. Add remaining ingredients except for parmesan cheese, heavy cream, and pesto and stir well.
5. Seal pot with lid and cook on high for 5 minutes.
6. Once done, release pressure using quick release. Remove lid.
7. Stir in parmesan cheese, heavy cream, and pesto and serve.

Nutrition Info:
- Calories 475 Fat 14.7 g Carbohydrates 57 g Sugar 2.8 g Protein 28.7 g Cholesterol 61 mg

Tortellini Salad With Broccoli

Servings: 12
Cooking Time: 20 Minutes

Ingredients:
- 1 red onion, chopped finely
- 1 cup sunflower seeds
- 1 cup raisins
- 3 heads fresh broccoli, cut into florets
- 2 tsp cider vinegar
- ½ cup white sugar
- ½ cup mayonnaise
- 20-oz fresh cheese filled tortellini

Directions:
1. In a large pot of boiling water, cook tortellini according to manufacturer's instructions. Drain and rinse with cold water and set aside.
2. Whisk vinegar, sugar and mayonnaise to create your salad dressing.
3. Mix together in a large bowl red onion, sunflower seeds, raisins, tortellini and broccoli. Pour dressing and toss to coat.
4. Serve and enjoy.

Nutrition Info:
- Calories per Serving: 272; Carbs: 38.7g; Protein: 5.0g; Fat: 8.1g

Mediterranean Diet Pasta With Mussels

Servings: 4
Cooking Time: 20 Minutes

Ingredients:

- 1 tbsp finely grated lemon zest
- ¼ cup chopped fresh parsley
- Freshly ground pepper to taste
- ¼ tsp salt
- Big pinch of crushed red pepper
- ¾ cup dry white wine
- 2 lbs. mussels, cleaned
- Big pinch of saffron threads soaked in 2 tbsp of water
- 1 can of 15 oz crushed tomatoes with basil
- 2 large cloves garlic, chopped
- ¼ cup extra virgin olive oil
- 8 oz whole wheat linguine or spaghetti

Directions:

1. Cook your pasta following the package label, drain and set aside while covering it to keep it warm.
2. On medium heat, place a large pan and heat oil. Sauté for two to three minutes the garlic and add the saffron plus liquid and the crushed tomatoes. Let it simmer for five minutes.
3. On high heat and in a different pot, boil the wine and mussels for four to six minutes or until it opens. Then transfer the mussels into a clean bowl while disposing of the unopened ones.
4. Then, with a sieve strain the mussel soup into the tomato sauce, add the red pepper and continue for a minute to simmer the sauce. Lastly, season with pepper and salt.
5. Then transfer half of the sauce into the pasta bowl and toss to mix. Then ladle the pasta into 4 medium sized serving bowls, top with mussels, remaining sauce, lemon zest and parsley in that order before serving.

Nutrition Info:

- Calories per Serving: 402; Carbs: 26.0g; Protein: 35.0g; Fat: 17.5g

Blue Cheese And Grains Salad

Servings: 4
Cooking Time: 40 Minutes

Ingredients:

- ¼ cup thinly sliced scallions
- ½ cup millet, rinsed
- ½ cup quinoa, rinsed
- 1 ½ tsp olive oil
- 1 Bartlett pear, cored and diced
- 1/8 tsp ground black pepper
- 2 cloves garlic, minced
- 2 oz blue cheese
- 2 tbsp fresh lemon juice
- 2 tsp dried rosemary
- 4 4-oz boneless, skinless chicken breasts
- 6 oz baby spinach
- olive oil cooking spray
- ¼ cup fresh raspberries
- 1 tbsp pure maple syrup
- 1 tsp fresh thyme leaf
- 2 tbsp grainy mustard
- 6 tbsp balsamic vinegar

Directions:

1. Bring millet, quinoa, and 2 ¼ cups water on a small saucepan to a boil. Once boiling, slow fire to a simmer and stir once. Cover and cook until water is fully absorbed and grains are soft around 15 minutes. Turn off fire, fluff grains with a fork and set aside to cool a bit.
2. Arrange one oven rack to highest position and preheat broiler. Line a baking sheet with foil, and grease with cooking spray.
3. Whisk well pepper, oil, rosemary, lemon juice and garlic. Rub onto chicken.
4. Place chicken on prepared pan, pop into the broiler and broil until juices run clear and no longer pin inside around 12 minutes.
5. Meanwhile, make the dressing by combining all ingredients in a blender. Blend until smooth.
6. Remove chicken from oven, cool slightly before cutting into strips, against the grain.
7. To assemble, place grains in a large salad bowl. Add in dressing and spinach, toss to mix well.
8. Add scallions and pear, mix gently and evenly divide into four plates. Top each salad with cheese and chicken.
9. Serve and enjoy.

Nutrition Info:

- Calories per Serving: 530.4; Carbs: 77g; Protein: 21.4g; Fat: 15.2g

Chickpea-crouton Kale Caesar Salad

Servings: 4
Cooking Time: 35 Minutes

Ingredients:

- 1 large bunch Tuscan kale, stem removed & thinly sliced
- ½ cup toasted pepitas
- 1 cup chickpeas, rinsed and drained
- 1 tbsp Dijon mustard
- 1 tbsp nutritional yeast
- 2 tbsp olive oil
- salt and pepper, to taste
- ½ cup silken tofu
- 2 tablespoons olive oil
- 1 lemon, zested and juiced
- 1 clove garlic
- 2 teaspoons capers, drained
- 2 tablespoons nutritional yeast
- 1 teaspoon Dijon mustard
- salt and pepper, to taste

Directions:

1. Heat oven to 350oF. Toss the chickpeas in the garlic, Dijon, nutritional yeast, olive oil, and salt and pepper. Roast for 30-35 minutes, until browned and crispy.
2. In a blender, add all dressing ingredients. Puree until smooth and creamy.
3. In a large salad bowl, toss the kale with dressing to taste, massaging lightly to tenderize the kale.
4. Top with the chickpea croutons, pepitas, and enjoy!

Nutrition Info:

- Calories per serving: 327; Protein: 11.9g; Carbs: 20.3g; Fat: 23.8g

Tasty Lasagna Rolls

Servings: 6
Cooking Time: 20 Minutes

Ingredients:

- ¼ tsp crushed red pepper
- ¼ tsp salt
- ½ cup shredded mozzarella cheese
- ½ cups parmesan cheese, shredded
- 1 14-oz package tofu, cubed
- 1 25-oz can of low-sodium marinara sauce
- 1 tbsp extra virgin olive oil
- 12 whole wheat lasagna noodles
- 2 tbsp Kalamata olives, chopped
- 3 cloves minced garlic
- 3 cups spinach, chopped

Directions:

1. Put enough water on a large pot and cook the lasagna noodles according to package instructions. Drain, rinse and set aside until ready to use.

2. In a large skillet, sauté garlic over medium heat for 20 seconds. Add the tofu and spinach and cook until the spinach wilts. Transfer this mixture in a bowl and add parmesan olives, salt, red pepper and 2/3 cup of the marinara sauce.

3. In a pan, spread a cup of marinara sauce on the bottom. To make the rolls, place noodle on a surface and spread ¼ cup of the tofu filling. Roll up and place it on the pan with the marinara sauce. Do this procedure until all lasagna noodles are rolled.

4. Place the pan over high heat and bring to a simmer. Reduce the heat to medium and let it cook for three more minutes. Sprinkle mozzarella cheese and let the cheese melt for two minutes. Serve hot.

Nutrition Info:

- Calories per Serving: 304; Carbs: 39.2g; Protein: 23g; Fat: 19.2g

Sun-dried Tomatoes And Chickpeas

Servings: 6
Cooking Time: 22 Minutes

Ingredients:

- 1 red bell pepper
- 1/2 cup parsley, chopped
- 1/4 cup red wine vinegar
- 2 14.5-ounce cans chickpeas, drained and rinsed
- 2 cloves garlic, chopped
- 2 cups water
- 2 tablespoons extra-virgin olive oil
- 4 sun-dried tomatoes
- Salt to taste

Directions:

1. Lengthwise, slice bell pepper in half. Place on baking sheet with skin side up. Broil on top rack for 5 minutes until skin is blistered.

2. In a brown paper bag, place the charred bell pepper halves. Fold bag and leave in there for 10 minutes. Remove pepper and peel off skin. Slice into thin strips.

3. Meanwhile, microwave 2 cups of water to boiling. Add the sun-dried tomatoes and leave in to reconstitute for 10 minutes. Drain and slice into thin strips.

4. Whisk well olive oil, garlic, and red wine vinegar.

5. Mix in parsley, sun-dried tomato, bell pepper, and chickpeas.

6. Season with salt to taste and serve.

Nutrition Info:

- Calories per serving: 195; Protein: 8.0g; Carbs: 26.0g; Fat: 7.0g

Kefta Styled Beef Patties With Cucumber Salad

Servings: 4
Cooking Time: 10 Minutes

Ingredients:

- 2 pcs of 6-inch pita, quartered
- ½ tsp freshly ground black pepper
- 1 tbsp fresh lemon juice
- ½ cup plain Greek yogurt, fat free
- 2 cups thinly sliced English cucumber
- ½ tsp ground cinnamon
- ½ tsp salt
- 1 tsp ground cumin
- 2 tsp ground coriander
- 1 tbsp peeled and chopped ginger
- ¼ cup cilantro, fresh
- ¼ cup plus 2 tbsp fresh parsley, chopped and divided
- 1 lb. ground sirloin

Directions:

1. On medium high fire, preheat a grill pan coated with cooking spray.
2. In a medium bowl, mix together cinnamon, salt, cumin, coriander, ginger, cilantro, parsley and beef. Then divide the mixture equally into four parts and shaping each portion into a patty ½ inch thick.
3. Then place patties on pan cooking each side for three minutes or until desired doneness is achieved.
4. In a separate bowl, toss together vinegar and cucumber.
5. In a small bowl, whisk together pepper, juice, 2 tbsp parsley and yogurt.
6. Serve each patty on a plate with ½ cup cucumber mixture and 2 tbsp of the yogurt sauce.

Nutrition Info:

- Calories per serving: 313; Carbs: 11.7g; Protein: 33.9g; Fat: 14.1g

Garlic Avocado-pesto And Zucchini Pasta

Servings: 2
Cooking Time: 0 Minutes

Ingredients:

- salt and pepper to taste
- 1 tbsp pine nuts
- 1 tbsp cashew nuts
- 1 lemon juice
- 4 cloves garlic, minced
- 1 small ripe avocado
- 2 cups zucchini, spiral
- 2 tbsp olive oil
- 2 tbsp grated Pecorino Cheese
- ½ cup packed fresh basil leaves

Directions:

1. In a food processor grind pine nuts and cashew nuts to a fine powder.
2. Add basil leaves, cheese, olive oil, ripe avocado, garlic, lemon juice, salt and pepper to taste and process until you have a smooth mixture.
3. Arrange zucchini pasta on two plates and top evenly with the Avocado pesto mixture.
4. Serve and enjoy.

Nutrition Info:

- Calories per Serving: 353; Carbs: 17.0g; Protein: 5.5g; Fat: 31.9g

Beans And Spinach Mediterranean Salad

Servings: 4
Cooking Time: 30 Minutes

Ingredients:

- 1 can (14 ounces) water-packed artichoke hearts, rinsed, drained and quartered
- 1 can (14-1/2 ounces) no-salt-added diced tomatoes, undrained
- 1 can (15 ounces) cannellini beans, rinsed and drained
- 1 small onion, chopped
- 1 tablespoon olive oil
- 1/4 teaspoon pepper
- 1/4 teaspoon salt
- 1/8 teaspoon crushed red pepper flakes
- 2 garlic cloves, minced
- 2 tablespoons Worcestershire sauce
- 6 ounces fresh baby spinach (about 8 cups)
- Additional olive oil, optional

Directions:

1. Place a saucepan on medium high fire and heat for a minute.
2. Add oil and heat for 2 minutes. Stir in onion and sauté for 4 minutes. Add garlic and sauté for another minute.
3. Stir in seasonings, Worcestershire sauce, and tomatoes. Cook for 5 minutes while stirring continuously until sauce is reduced.
4. Stir in spinach, artichoke hearts, and beans. Sauté for 3 minutes until spinach is wilted and other ingredients are heated through.
5. Serve and enjoy.

Nutrition Info:

- Calories per serving: 187; Protein: 8.0g; Carbs: 30.0g; Fat: 4.0g

Delicious Chicken Pasta

Servings: 4
Cooking Time: 17 Minutes

Ingredients:
- 3 chicken breasts, skinless, boneless, cut into pieces
- 9 oz whole-grain pasta
- 1/2 cup olives, sliced
- 1/2 cup sun-dried tomatoes
- 1 tbsp roasted red peppers, chopped
- 14 oz can tomatoes, diced
- 2 cups marinara sauce
- 1 cup chicken broth
- Pepper
- Salt

Directions:
1. Add all ingredients except whole-grain pasta into the instant pot and stir well.
2. Seal pot with lid and cook on high for 12 minutes.
3. Once done, allow to release pressure naturally. Remove lid.
4. Add pasta and stir well. Seal pot again and select manual and set timer for 5 minutes.
5. Once done, allow to release pressure naturally for 5 minutes then release remaining using quick release. Remove lid.
6. Stir well and serve.

Nutrition Info:
- Calories 615 Fat 15.4 g Carbohydrates 71 g Sugar 17.6 g Protein 48 g Cholesterol 100 mg

Black Beans And Quinoa

Servings: 6
Cooking Time: 30 Minutes

Ingredients:
- ½ cup chopped cilantro
- 2 15-oz cans black beans, rinsed and drained
- 1 cup frozen corn kernels
- Pepper and salt to taste
- ¼ tsp cayenne pepper
- 1 tsp ground cumin
- 1 ½ cups vegetable broth
- ¾ cup quinoa
- 3 cloves garlic, chopped
- 1 onion, chopped
- 1 tsp vegetable oil

Directions:
1. On medium fire, place a saucepan and heat oil.
2. Add garlic and onions. Sauté for 5 minutes or until onions are soft.
3. Add quinoa. Pour vegetable broth and bring to a boil while increasing fire.

4. As you wait for broth to boil, season quinoa mixture with pepper, salt, cayenne pepper, and cumin.
5. Once boiling, reduce fire to a simmer, cover and simmer around 20 minutes or until liquid is fully absorbed.
6. Once liquid is fully absorbed, stir in black beans and frozen corn. Continue cooking until heated through, around 5 minutes.
7. To serve, add cilantro, toss well to mix, and enjoy.

Nutrition Info:
- Calories per serving: 262; Carbs: 47.1g; Protein: 13.0g; Fat: 2.9g

Mexican Quinoa Bake

Servings: 4
Cooking Time: 40 Minutes

Ingredients:
- 3 cups sweet potato, peeled, diced very small (about 1 large sweet potato)
- 2 cups cooked quinoa
- 1 cup shredded sharp cheddar cheese
- 2 Tbs chili powder
- T Tbs paprika
- 1 1/4 cup salsa of your choice
- 1 red bell pepper, diced
- 1 large carrot, diced
- 3 Tbs canned green chiles
- 1 small onion, diced
- 3 garlic cloves, minced
- 2 cups cooked black beans

Directions:
1. Preheat oven to 400oF.
2. Dice, chop, measure and prep all ingredients.
3. Combine all ingredients in one big bowl and toss ingredients well.
4. Spray a 9 X 13-inch pan with cooking spray and pour all ingredients in.
5. Bake for 35-40 minutes or until sweet potato pieces are slightly mushy, cheese is melted and items are heated all the way through.
6. Let sit for about 5 minutes, scoop into bowls and enjoy!

Nutrition Info:
- Calories per serving: 414; Carbs: 56.6g; Protein: 22.0g; Fat: 13.0g

Grilled Veggie And Pasta With Marinara Sauce

Servings: 4
Cooking Time: 30 Minutes

Ingredients:
- 8 oz whole wheat spaghetti
- 1 sweet onion, sliced into ¼-inch wide rounds
- 1 zucchini, sliced lengthwise
- 1 yellow summer squash, sliced lengthwise
- 2 red peppers, sliced into chunks
- 1/8 tsp freshly ground black pepper
- ½ tsp dried oregano
- 1 tsp sugar
- 1 tbsp chopped fresh basil or 1 tsp dried basil
- 2 tbsp chopped onion
- ½ tsp minced garlic
- salt
- 10 large fresh tomatoes, peeled and diced
- 2 tbsp extra virgin olive oil, divided

Directions:
1. Make the marinara sauce by heating on medium high fire a tablespoon of oil in a large fry pan.
2. Sauté black pepper, oregano, sugar, basil, onions, garlic, salt and tomatoes. Once simmering, lower fire and allow to simmer for 30 minutes or until sauce has thickened.
3. Meanwhile, preheat broiler and grease baking pan with cooking spray.
4. Add sweet onion, zucchini, squash and red peppers in baking pan and brush with oil. Broil for 5 to 8 minutes or until vegetables are tender. Remove from oven and transfer veggies into a bowl.
5. Bring a large pot of water to a boil. Once boiling, add pasta and cook following manufacturer's instructions. Once al dente, drain and divide equally into 4 plates.
6. To serve, equally divide marinara sauce on to pasta, top with grilled veggies and enjoy.

Nutrition Info:
- Calories per Serving: ; Carbs: 41.9g; Protein: 8.3g; Fat: 6.2g

Flavors Taco Rice Bowl

Servings: 8
Cooking Time: 14 Minutes

Ingredients:
- 1 lb ground beef
- 8 oz cheddar cheese, shredded
- 14 oz can red beans
- 2 oz taco seasoning
- 16 oz salsa
- 2 cups of water
- 2 cups brown rice
- Pepper
- Salt

Directions:
1. Set instant pot on sauté mode.
2. Add meat to the pot and sauté until brown.
3. Add water, beans, rice, taco seasoning, pepper, and salt and stir well.
4. Top with salsa. Seal pot with lid and cook on high for 14 minutes.
5. Once done, release pressure using quick release. Remove lid.
6. Add cheddar cheese and stir until cheese is melted.
7. Serve and enjoy.

Nutrition Info:
- Calories 464 Fat 15.3 g Carbohydrates 48.9 g Sugar 2.8 g Protein 32.2 g Cholesterol 83 mg

Pecorino Pasta With Sausage And Fresh Tomato

Servings: 4
Cooking Time: 20 Minutes

Ingredients:
- ¼ cup torn fresh basil leaves
- 1/8 tsp black pepper
- ¼ tsp salt
- 6 tbsp grated fresh pecorino Romano cheese, divided
- 1 ¼ lbs. tomatoes, chopped
- 2 tsp minced garlic
- 1 cup vertically sliced onions
- 2 tsp olive oil
- 8 oz sweet Italian sausage
- 8 oz uncooked penne, cooked and drained

Directions:
1. On medium high fire, place a nonstick fry pan with oil and cook for five minutes onion and sausage. Stir constantly to break sausage into pieces.
2. Stir in garlic and continue cooking for two minutes more.
3. Add tomatoes and cook for another two minutes.
4. Remove pan from fire, season with pepper and salt. Mix well.
5. Stir in 2 tbsp cheese and pasta. Toss well.
6. Transfer to a serving dish, garnish with basil and remaining cheese before serving.

Nutrition Info:
- Calories per Serving: 376; Carbs: 50.8g; Protein: 17.8g; Fat: 11.6g

Pesto Pasta And Shrimps

Servings: 4
Cooking Time: 15 Minutes

Ingredients:
- ¼ cup pesto, divided
- ¼ cup shaved Parmesan Cheese
- 1 ¼ lbs. large shrimp, peeled and deveined
- 1 cup halved grape tomatoes
- 4-oz angel hair pasta, cooked, rinsed and drained

Directions:
1. On medium high fire, place a nonstick large fry pan and grease with cooking spray.
2. Add tomatoes, pesto and shrimp. Cook for 15 minutes or until shrimps are opaque, while covered.
3. Stir in cooked pasta and cook until heated through.
4. Transfer to a serving plate and garnish with Parmesan cheese.

Nutrition Info:
- Calories per Serving: 319; Carbs: 23.6g; Protein: 31.4g; Fat: 11g

Orange, Dates And Asparagus On Quinoa Salad

Servings: 8
Cooking Time: 25 Minutes

Ingredients:
- ¼ cup chopped pecans, toasted
- ½ cup white onion, finely chopped
- ½ jalapeno pepper, diced
- ½ lb. asparagus, sliced into 2-inch lengths, steamed and chilled
- ½ tsp salt
- 1 cup fresh orange sections
- 1 cup uncooked quinoa
- 1 tsp olive oil
- 2 cups water
- 2 tbsp minced red onion
- 5 dates, pitted and chopped
- ¼ tsp freshly ground black pepper
- ¼ tsp salt
- 1 garlic clove, minced
- 1 tbsp extra virgin olive oil
- 2 tbsp chopped fresh mint
- 2 tbsp fresh lemon juice
- Mint sprigs – optional

Directions:
1. On medium high fire, place a large nonstick pan and heat 1 tsp oil.
2. Add white onion and sauté for two minutes.
3. Add quinoa and for 5 minutes sauté it.
4. Add salt and water. Bring to a boil, once boiling, slow fire to a simmer and cook for 15 minutes while covered.
5. Turn off fire and leave for 15 minutes, to let quinoa absorb the remaining water.
6. Transfer quinoa to a large salad bowl. Add jalapeno pepper, asparagus, dates, red onion, pecans and oranges. Toss to combine.
7. Make the dressing by mixing garlic, pepper, salt, olive oil and lemon juice in a small bowl.
8. Pour dressing into quinoa salad along with chopped mint, mix well.
9. If desired, garnish with mint sprigs before serving.

Nutrition Info:
- Calories per Serving: 265.2; Carbs: 28.3g; Protein: 14.6g; Fat: 10.4g

Kidney Beans And Beet Salad

Servings: 4
Cooking Time: 15 Minutes

Ingredients:
- 1 14.5-ounce can kidney beans, drained and rinsed
- 1 tablespoon pomegranate syrup or juice
- 2 tablespoons olive oil
- 4 beets, scrubbed and stems removed
- 4 green onions, chopped
- Juice of 1 lemon
- Salt and pepper to taste

Directions:
1. Bring a pot of water to boil and add beets. Simmer for 10 minutes or until tender. Drain beets and place in ice bath for 5 minutes.
2. Peel bets and slice in halves.
3. Toss to mix the pomegranate syrup, olive oil, lemon juice, green onions, and kidney beans in a salad bowl.
4. Stir in beets. Season with pepper and salt to taste.
5. Serve and enjoy.

Nutrition Info:
- Calories per serving: 175; Protein: 6.0g; Carbs: 22.0g; Fat: 7.0g

Lentils And Rice (mujaddara With Rice)

Serves: 1 Cup
Cooking Time:1 Hour 10 Minutes

Ingredients:
- 1/4 cup extra-virgin olive oil
- 1 large yellow onion, finely chopped
- 2 tsp. salt
- 2 cups green or brown lentils, picked over and rinsed
- 6 cups water
- 1 cup long-grain rice or brown rice
- 1 TB. cumin

Directions:
1. In a large, 3-quart pot over medium-low heat, heat extra-virgin olive oil. Add yellow onion and 1 teaspoon salt, and cook, stirring intermittently, for 10 minutes.
2. Add green lentils and water, and cook, stirring intermittently, for 20 minutes.
3. Stir in long-grain rice, remaining 1 teaspoon salt, and cumin. Cover and cook, stirring intermittently, for 40 minutes.
4. Serve warm or at room temperature with tzatziki sauce or a Mediterranean salad.

Turkey And Quinoa Stuffed Peppers

Servings: 6
Cooking Time: 55 Minutes

Ingredients:
- 3 large red bell peppers
- 2 tsp chopped fresh rosemary
- 2 tbsp chopped fresh parsley
- 3 tbsp chopped pecans, toasted
- ¼ cup extra virgin olive oil
- ½ cup chicken stock
- ½ lb. fully cooked smoked turkey sausage, diced
- ½ tsp salt
- 2 cups water
- 1 cup uncooked quinoa

Directions:
1. On high fire, place a large saucepan and add salt, water and quinoa. Bring to a boil.
2. Once boiling, reduce fire to a simmer, cover and cook until all water is absorbed around 15 minutes.
3. Uncover quinoa, turn off fire and let it stand for another 5 minutes.
4. Add rosemary, parsley, pecans, olive oil, chicken stock and turkey sausage into pan of quinoa. Mix well.
5. Slice peppers lengthwise in half and discard membranes and seeds. In another boiling pot of water, add peppers, boil for 5 minutes, drain and discard water.
6. Grease a 13 x 9 baking dish and preheat oven to 350oF.
7. Place boiled bell pepper onto prepared baking dish, evenly fill with the quinoa mixture and pop into oven.

8. Bake for 15 minutes.

Nutrition Info:
- Calories per Serving: 255.6; Carbs: 21.6g; Protein: 14.4g; Fat: 12.4g

Chicken And White Bean

Servings: 8
Cooking Time: 70 Minutes

Ingredients:
- 2 tbsp fresh cilantro, chopped
- 2 cups grated Monterey Jack cheese
- 3 cups water
- 1/8 tsp cayenne pepper
- 2 tsp pure chile powder
- 2 tsp ground cumin
- 1 4-oz can chopped green chiles
- 1 cup corn kernels
- 2 15-oz cans shite beans, drained and rinsed
- 2 garlic cloves
- 1 medium onion, diced
- 2 tbsp extra virgin olive oil
- 1 lb. chicken breasts, boneless and skinless

Directions:
1. Slice chicken breasts into ½-inch cubes and with pepper and salt, season it.
2. On high fire, place a large nonstick fry pan and heat oil.
3. Sauté chicken pieces for three to four minutes or until lightly browned.
4. Reduce fire to medium and add garlic and onion.
5. Cook for 5 to 6 minutes or until onions are translucent.
6. Add water, spices, chilies, corn and beans. Bring to a boil.
7. Once boiling, slow fire to a simmer and continue simmering for an hour, uncovered.
8. To serve, garnish with a sprinkling of cilantro and a tablespoon of cheese.

Nutrition Info:
- Calories per serving: 433; Protein: 30.6g; Carbs: 29.5g; Fat: 21.8g

Salads & Side Dishes Recipes

Salads & Side Dishes Recipes

Lettuce And Cucumber Salad

Servings: 4
Cooking Time: 0 Minutes

Ingredients:

- 2 tablespoons olive oil
- 2 cucumbers, sliced
- 1 romaine lettuce head, torn
- 1 medium tomato, chopped
- ½ teaspoon sumac
- 1 cup parsley, chopped
- Juice of 1 lime

Directions:

1. In a bowl, mix the cucumbers with the lettuce and the rest of the ingredients, toss and serve.

Nutrition Info:

- calories 133, fat 5.1, fiber 1.1, carbs 1.3, protein 4.4

Quinoa And Greens Salad

Servings: 4
Cooking Time: 0 Minutes

Ingredients:

- 1 cup quinoa, cooked
- 1 medium bunch collard greens, chopped
- 4 tablespoons walnuts, chopped
- 2 tablespoons balsamic vinegar
- 4 tablespoons tahini paste
- 4 tablespoons cold water
- A pinch of salt and black pepper
- 1 tablespoon olive oil

Directions:

1. In a bowl, mix the tahini with the water and vinegar and whisk.
2. In a bowl, mix the quinoa with the rest of the ingredients and the tahini dressing, toss, divide the mix between plates and serve as a side dish.

Nutrition Info:

- calories 175, fat 3, fiber 3, carbs 5, protein 3

Prosciutto And Pea Soup

Servings: 6
Cooking Time:15 Minutes

Ingredients:

- 600 g (about 4 cups) frozen peas
- 3 tablespoons olive oil
- 2 vegetable stock cubes
- 2 garlic cloves, crushed
- 125 g (about 1/2 cup) light sour cream
- 100 g prosciutto
- 1.25 liters (about 5 cups) water
- 1 leek, trimmed, halved lengthways, and thinly sliced

Directions:

1. In a frying pan, heat 1 tablespoon of the olive oil over medium-high heat. Add ½ of the prosciutto; cook for 1 minute per side or until crispy; transfer to a plate, break into large pieces, and reserve.
2. In a large saucepan, heat the remaining olive oil over medium heat. Coarsely chop the remaining prosciutto; add to the pan. Add the garlic and leek; cook, for 3 minutes, stirring, or until soft.
3. Add the water and the vegetable stock cubes; bring to a boil.
4. Add the peas; cook for 5 minutes, stirring occasionally, or until just cooked. Set aside and let cool slightly for 5 minutes.
5. Pour 1/3 of the pea mixture in a blender and process until smooth; transfer into a clean saucepan. Repeat the process with the remaining mixture, blending in 2 batches. Over medium heat, heat for 2 minutes or until heated through; season with the salt and pepper.
6. Divide the soup between serving bowls; top with the sour cream and the reserved prosciutto. Serve with garlic bread.

Nutrition Info:

- Per Serving:366.2 cal., 26 g total fat (7 g sat. fat), 6 g sugar, 17 g carb., 7 g fiber, 13 g protein, 21 mg chol., and 790.37 mg sodium.

Chicken Cabbage Soup

Servings: 8
Cooking Time: 35 Minutes

Ingredients:

- 2celery stalks
- 2garlic cloves, minced
- 4 oz.butter
- 6 oz. mushrooms, sliced
- 2 tablespoons onions, dried and minced
- 1 teaspoon salt
- 8 cups chicken broth
- 1medium carrot
- 2 cups green cabbage, sliced into strips
- 2 teaspoons dried parsley
- ¼ teaspoon black pepper
- 1½ rotisserie chickens, shredded

Directions:

1. Melt butter in a large pot and add celery, mushrooms, onions and garlic into the pot.
2. Cook for about 4 minutes and add broth, parsley, carrot, salt and black pepper.
3. Simmer for about 10 minutes and add cooked chicken and cabbage.
4. Simmer for an additional 12 minutes until the cabbage is tender.
5. Dish out and serve hot.

Nutrition Info:
- Calories: 184 Carbs: 4.2g Fats: 13.1g Proteins: 12.6g Sodium: 1244mg Sugar: 2.1g

Fresh And Light Cabbage Salad

Servings: 4
Cooking Time: 25 Minutes

Ingredients:
- Mint - 1 tbsp., chopped
- Ground coriander - 1 2 tsp.
- Savoy cabbage - 1, shredded
- Greek yogurt - 1 2 cup
- Cumin seeds - 1 4 tsp.
- Extra virgin olive oil - 2 tbsp.
- Carrot - 1, grated
- Red onion – 1, sliced
- Honey - 1 tsp.
- Lemon zest - 1 tsp.
- Lemon juice - 2 tbsp.
- Salt and pepper - to taste

Directions:
1. In a salad bowl, mix all Ingredients
2. You can add salt and pepper to suit your taste and then mix again.
3. This salad is best when cool and freshly made.

Tuna-mediterranean Salad

Servings: 6
Cooking Time: 0 Minutes

Ingredients:
- ¼ cup chopped pitted ripe olives
- ¼ cup drained and chopped roasted red peppers
- ¼ cup Mayonnaise dressing with olive oil
- 1 tbsp small capers, rinsed and drained
- 2 green onions, sliced
- 2 pcs of 6 oz cans of tuna, drained and flaked
- 6 slices whole wheat bread optional
- Salad greens like lettuce optional

Directions:
1. With the exception of salad greens or bread, mix together all of the ingredients in a bowl. If desired, you can arrange it on top of salad greens or serve with bread

Nutrition Info:

- Calories per Serving: 197.1; Protein: 6.9g; Fat: 5.7g; Carbs: 16.3g

Buffalo Ranch Chicken Soup

Servings: 4
Cooking Time: 40 Minutes

Ingredients:
- 2 tablespoons parsley
- 2 celery stalks, chopped
- 6 tablespoons butter
- 1 cup heavy whipping cream
- 4 cups chicken, cooked and shredded
- 4 tablespoons ranch dressing
- ¼ cup yellow onions, chopped
- 8 oz cream cheese
- 8 cups chicken broth
- 7 hearty bacon slices, crumbled

Directions:
1. Heat butter in a pan and add chicken.
2. Cook for about 5 minutes and add 1½ cups water.
3. Cover and cook for about 10 minutes.
4. Put the chicken and rest of the ingredients into the saucepan except parsley and cook for about 10 minutes.
5. Top with parsley and serve hot.

Nutrition Info:
- Calories: 444 Carbs: 4g Fats: 34g Proteins: 28g Sodium: 1572mg Sugar: 2g

Fruity Salad

Servings: 4
Cooking Time:20 Minutes

Ingredients:
- 8 oz. seedless watermelon, cubed
- 4 oz. red grapes, halved
- 1 cup strawberries, halved
- 2 cucumbers, sliced
- 2 cups arugula
- 6 oz. feta cheese, cubed
- 2 tablespoons balsamic vinegar

Directions:
1. Combine the watermelon, grapes, strawberries, cucumbers, arugula and feta cheese in a salad bowl.
2. Drizzle with vinegar and serve the salad as fresh as possible.

Nutrition Info:
- Per Serving:Calories:166 Fat:9.5g Protein:7.8g Carbohydrates:14.6g

Grilled Salmon Bulgur Salad

Servings: 4
Cooking Time:30 Minutes

Ingredients:

- 2 salmon fillets
- Salt and pepper to taste
- ½ cup bulgur
- 2 cups vegetable stock
- 1 cup cherry tomatoes, halved
- 1 cucumber, cubed
- 1 green onion, chopped
- ½ cup green olives, sliced
- 1 red bell pepper, cored and diced
- 1 red pepper, chopped
- ½ cup sweet corn
- 1 lemon, juiced

Directions:

1. Season the salmon with salt and pepper and place it on a hot grill pan. Cook it on each side until browned.
2. Combine the bulgur and stock in a saucepan. Cook until all the liquid has been absorbed then transfer in a salad bowl.
3. Add the rest of the ingredients, including the salmon and season with salt and pepper.
4. Serve the salad fresh.

Nutrition Info:

- Per Serving:Calories:239 Fat:6.3g Protein:21.8g Carbohydrates:27.2g

Sweet And Sour Spinach Red Onion Salad

Servings: 4
Cooking Time:15 Minutes

Ingredients:

- 4 baby spinach leaves
- 2 red onions, sliced
- 2 tablespoons apple cider vinegar
- 1 teaspoon honey
- ½ teaspoon sesame oil
- Salt and pepper to taste
- 2 tablespoons sesame seeds

Directions:

1. Combine the spinach and red onions in a salad bowl.
2. For the dressing, mix the vinegar, honey, sesame oil, sesame seeds, salt and pepper in a bowl.
3. Drizzle the dressing over the salad and serve it as fresh as possible.

Nutrition Info:

- Per Serving: Calories:62 Fat:2.9g Protein:1.7g Carbohydrates:8.1g

Orange Potato Salad

Servings: 4
Cooking Time: 40 Minutes

Ingredients:

- 4 sweet potatoes
- 3 tablespoons olive oil
- 1/3 cup orange juice
- ½ teaspoon sumac, ground
- 1 tablespoon red wine vinegar
- Salt and black pepper to the taste
- 1 tablespoon orange zest, grated
- 2 tablespoons mint, chopped
- 1/3 cup walnuts, chopped
- 1/3 cup pomegranate seeds

Directions:

1. Put the potatoes on a lined baking sheet, introduce them in the oven at 350 degrees F, bake for 40 minutes, cool them down, peel, cut into wedges and transfer to a bowl.
2. Add the rest of the ingredients, toss, and serve cold.

Nutrition Info:

- calories 138, fat 3.5, fiber 6.2, carbs 10.4, protein 6.5

Grilled Vegetable And Orzo Salad With Olives, Feta, And Oregano

Servings:4-6
Cooking Time:15 Minutes

Ingredients:

- 1 medium red bell pepper, quartered, stemmed, seeded
- 1 tablespoon Dijon mustard
- 1/2 cup feta, crumbled (2 1/2 ounce)
- 1/2 cup Kalamata olives, pitted, coarsely chopped
- 1/2 small red onion (about 2/3 cup), cut into small dice
- 1/3 cup extra-virgin olive oil, plus 2 tablespoons
- 2 small Italian eggplants (about 3/4 lb. total), sliced into 1/2-inch-thick rounds
- 2 tablespoons red-wine vinegar
- 3 tablespoons chopped fresh oregano
- 8 ounces (1 1/4 cups) orzo
- Kosher salt
- Vegetable oil, for the grill

Directions:

1. In a 4-quart saucepan, bring a 2-quart worth of water to a boil over high heat. Add 1 tablespoon salt. Add the orzo; cook for about 8 minutes, stirring occasionally, or until just tender (or follow package directions). Drain, don't rinse, and pour into a rimmed baking sheet to quickly and evenly cool.
2. Preheat the gas grill burners on high. Clean the grate and grease with the oil.
3. In a bowl, toss the eggplant and the bell pepper with 2 tablespoons oil and a generous sprinkle of salt. Place the

vegetables of the grill; cook, covered, for about 2-3 minutes per side or until cooked through and grill marks appear. Transfer to a cutting board, let cool slightly, and cut into small dice pieces.

4. In a liquid measuring cup, whisk the mustard, vinegar, and generous pinch of salt. Whisk in the remaining 1/3 cup olive oil slowly into the mustard mixture.

5. When ready to serve, combine the grilled vegetables, orzo, feta, onion, oregano, and olives in a medium-sized bowl. Pour the dressing, toss well, and serve.

Nutrition Info:
- per serving:380 cal., 23 g fat (4.5 g sat. fat, 15 g mono fat, 2.5 g poly fat), 8 g protein, 36 g carb., 4 g fiber, 10 mg chol., and 450 mg sodium.

Lemony Lentil Salad With Salmon

Servings: 6
Cooking Time: 0 Minutes

Ingredients:
- ¼ tsp salt
- ½ cup chopped red onion
- 1 cup diced seedless cucumber
- 1 medium red bell pepper, diced
- 1/3 cup extra virgin olive oil
- 1/3 cup fresh dill, chopped
- 1/3 cup lemon juice
- 2 15oz cans of lentils
- 2 7oz cans of salmon, drained and flaked
- 2 tsp Dijon mustard
- Pepper to taste

Directions:
1. In a bowl, mix together, lemon juice, mustard, dill, salt and pepper.
2. Gradually add the oil, bell pepper, onion, cucumber, salmon flakes and lentils.
3. Toss to coat evenly.

Nutrition Info:
- Calories per serving: 349.1; Protein: 27.1g; Carbs: 35.2g; Fat: 11.1g

Mushroom Risotto

Servings: 4
Cooking Time: 55 Minutes

Ingredients:
- 1 cup farro
- 4 cups chicken stock
- 2 oz Parmesan, shaved
- 1 teaspoon ground thyme
- 1 teaspoon ground black pepper
- ½ teaspoon chili flakes
- ½ teaspoon paprika
- ½ teaspoon ground coriander
- 1 teaspoon dried oregano
- 1 tablespoon butter
- 1 yellow onion, diced
- ½ cup cremini mushrooms, sliced
- ¼ cup heavy cream

Directions:
1. Toss butter in the saucepan and heat it up.
2. Add onion and mushrooms. Saute the vegetables for 10 minutes over the medium heat.
3. Then sprinkle them with ground thyme, ground black pepper, chili flakes, paprika, ground coriander, and dried oregano. Mix up well.
4. After this, add the farro and roast the ingredients for 5 minutes. Stir them from time to time with the help of a spatula.
5. Then add heavy cream, chicken stock, and Parmesan. Mix up well and close the lid.
6. Saute risotto for 40 minutes over the medium-low heat.

Nutrition Info:
- Per Servingcalories 164, fat 9.4, fiber 1.9, carbs 13.5, protein 7.9

Dill Eggplants

Servings: 4
Cooking Time: 18 Minutes

Ingredients:
- 1 cup Plain yogurt
- 1 tablespoon butter
- 1 teaspoon ground black pepper
- 1 teaspoon salt
- 2 eggplants, chopped
- 1 tablespoon fresh dill, chopped

Directions:
1. Heat up butter in the skillet.
2. Toss eggplants in the hot butter. Sprinkle them with salt and ground black pepper.
3. Roast the vegetables for 5 minutes over the medium-high heat. Stir them from time to time.
4. After this, add fresh dill and Plain Yogurt. Mix up well.
5. Close the lid and simmer eggplants for 10 minutes more over the medium-high heat.

Nutrition Info:
- Per Servingcalories 141, fat 4.2, fiber 9.9, carbs 21.2, protein 6.4

Spinach And Grilled Feta Salad

Servings: 6
Cooking Time: 20 Minutes

Ingredients:
- Feta cheese - 8 oz., sliced
- Black olives - 1 4 cup, sliced
- Green olives - 1 4 cup, sliced
- Baby spinach - 4 cups
- Garlic cloves - 2, minced
- Capers - 1 tsp., chopped
- Extra virgin olive oil - 2 tbsp.
- Red wine vinegar - 1 tbsp.

Directions:
1. Grill feta cheese slices over medium to high flame until brown on both sides.
2. In a salad bowl, mix green olives, black olives and spinach.
3. In a separate bowl, mix vinegar, capers and oil together to make a dressing.
4. Top salad with the dressing and cheese and it's is ready to serve.

Lemony Carrots

Servings: 4
Cooking Time: 40 Minutes

Ingredients:
- 3 tablespoons olive oil
- 2 pounds baby carrots, trimmed
- Salt and black pepper to the taste
- ½ teaspoon lemon zest, grated
- 1 tablespoon lemon juice
- 1/3 cup Greek yogurt
- 1 garlic clove, minced
- 1 teaspoon cumin, ground
- 1 tablespoon dill, chopped

Directions:
1. In a roasting pan, combine the carrots with the oil, salt, pepper and the rest of the ingredients except the dill, toss and bake at 400 degrees F for 20 minutes.
2. Reduce the temperature to 375 degrees F and cook for 20 minutes more.
3. Divide the mix between plates, sprinkle the dill on top and serve.

Nutrition Info:
- calories 192, fat 5.4, fiber 3.4, carbs 7.3, protein 5.6

Fig Salad

Serves: 2 Cups
Cooking Time:15 Minutes

Ingredients:
- 2 cups dried figs
- 2 cups hot water
- 2 cups water
- 1 cup bulgur wheat, grind #2
- 6 cups fresh arugula
- 1 cup plain walnuts
- 2 TB. honey
- 3 TB. red wine vinegar
- 3 TB. extra-virgin olive oil
- 1/2 tsp. salt
- 1/2 tsp. fresh ground black pepper

Directions:
1. In a medium bowl, add figs. Pour hot water over figs, set aside to soak for 30 minutes, and drain. Cut figs into quarters.
2. In a large saucepan over medium heat, bring 2 cups water to a boil. Add bulgur wheat, reduce heat to low, cover, and cook for 15 minutes or until all of water is absorbed. Fluff with a fork, and let cool.
3. In a large bowl, add arugula, figs, bulgur wheat, and walnuts.
4. In a small bowl, whisk together honey, red wine vinegar, extra-virgin olive oil, salt, and black pepper.
5. Pour dressing over arugula mixture, and toss to coat.
6. Serve immediately.

Cucumber Greek Yoghurt Salad

Serves:6
Cooking Time: 0 Minutes

Ingredients:
- 4tbsp Greek yoghurt
- 4 large cucumbers peeled seeded and sliced
- 1 tbsp dried dill
- 1 tbsp apple cider vinegar
- 1/4 tsp garlic powder
- 1/4 tsp ground black pepper
- 1/2 tsp sugar
- 1/2 tsp salt

Directions:
1. Place all the Ingredients leaving out the cucumber into a bowl and whisk this until all is incorporated. Add your cucumber slices and toss until all is well mixed.
2. Let the salad chill 10 minutes in the refrigerator and then serve.

Avocado And Mushroom Mix

Servings: 4
Cooking Time: 10 Minutes

Ingredients:
- 1 yellow onion, chopped
- 1 tablespoon balsamic vinegar
- 2 tablespoons olive oil
- 12 ounces mushrooms, sliced
- 2 avocados, pitted, peeled and cubed
- 1 garlic clove, minced
- A pinch of salt and black pepper

Directions:
1. Heat up a pan with half of the oil over medium-high heat, add the mushrooms, sauté for 10 minutes and transfer to a bowl.
2. Add the rest of the ingredients, toss and serve.

Nutrition Info:
- calories 187, fat 4.3, fiber 4.2, carbs 11.6, protein 4

Bacon And Tomato Pasta

Servings: 4
Cooking Time: 20 Minutes

Ingredients:
- 1 egg, beaten
- 4 oz linguine
- 1 oz bacon, chopped
- ½ teaspoon canola oil
- 1 cup cherry tomatoes, halved
- 1 oz Romano cheese, grated
- 1 oz shallot, chopped
- 2 cups of water

Directions:
1. Pour water in the pan and bring to boil.
2. Add linguine and cook it according to the directions of the manufacturer.
3. When the linguine is cooked, drain ½ part of water.
4. Put bacon in the skillet, add canola oil, and roast it for 5 minutes or until crunchy.
5. Add cooked bacon in the linguine.
6. Then add shallot, grated Romano cheese, cherry tomatoes, and beaten egg.
7. Mix up the pasta carefully until it is homogenous and egg is dissolved.
8. Simmer pasta for 3 minutes over the medium-low heat.

Nutrition Info:
- Per Servingcalories 182, fat 7.3, fiber 0.5, carbs 18.9, protein 10.1

Watermelon-cucumber Salsa With Olives

Servings: 4
Cooking Time: 15 Minutes

Ingredients:
- 1 Lebanese cucumber, ends trimmed, cut into 1-cm thick pieces
- 1/2 cup fresh mint leaves, torn
- 1/4 red onion, cut into 1-cm thick pieces
- 100g feta, crumbled
- 2 teaspoons extra-virgin olive oil
- 2 teaspoons red wine vinegar
- 55 g (about 1/3 cup) Kalamata olives, pitted, cut into 1-cm thick pieces
- 650 g seedless watermelon, rind removed, cut into 1-cm thick pieces
- Barbecued fish or chicken, to serve

Directions:
1. In a large-sized bowl, place the cucumber, watermelon, olives, and onion; season with the salt and pepper. Add the mint and the feta; toss gently to combine.
2. In a bowl, combine the vinegar and the oil; pour over the watermelon mixture. Divide into serving plates with your favorite barbecued chicken or fish.

Nutrition Info:
- Per Serving:142 cal, 10 g total fat (4.5 g sat. fat), 7 g carb, 5.50 g protein, and 1.5 g fiber.

Blue Cheese And Arugula Salad

Servings: 4
Cooking Time: 0 Minutes

Ingredients:
- ¼ cup crumbled blue cheese
- 1 tsp Dijon mustard
- 1-pint fresh figs, quartered
- 2 bags arugula
- 3 tbsp Balsamic Vinegar
- 3 tbsp olive oil
- Pepper and salt to taste

Directions:
1. Whisk thoroughly together pepper, salt, olive oil, Dijon mustard, and balsamic vinegar to make the dressing. Set aside in the ref for at least 30 minutes to marinate and allow the spices to combine.
2. On four serving plates, evenly arrange arugula and top with blue cheese and figs.
3. Drizzle each plate of salad with 1 ½ tbsp of prepared dressing.
4. Serve and enjoy.

Nutrition Info:
- Calories per serving: 202; Protein: 2.5g; Carbs: 25.5g; Fat: 10g

Meat Recipes

Meat Recipes

Easy Stir-fried Chicken

Servings: 3
Cooking Time: 12 Minutes

Ingredients:

- ¼ lb. brown mushrooms
- ¼ medium onion, sliced thinly
- 1 large orange bell pepper
- 1 tbsp soy sauce
- 1 tbsp virgin coconut oil
- 2 7-oz skinless and boneless chicken breast

Directions:

1. On medium high fire, place a nonstick saucepan and heat coconut oil.
2. Add soy sauce, onion powder, mushrooms, bell pepper and chicken.
3. Stir fry for 8 to 10 minutes.
4. Remove from pan and serve.

Nutrition Info:

- Calories per Serving: 184; Carbs: 7.0g; Protein: 32.0g; Fat: 10.0g

Thyme Pork And Pearl Onions

Servings: 4
Cooking Time: 45 Minutes

Ingredients:

- 2 pounds pork loin roast, boneless and cubed
- 2 tablespoons olive oil
- Salt and black pepper to the taste
- 1 cup tomato sauce
- 2 garlic cloves, minced
- 1 teaspoon thyme, chopped
- ¾ pound pearl onions, peeled

Directions:

1. In a roasting pan, combine the pork with the oil and the rest of the ingredients, toss, introduce in the oven and bake at 380 degrees F for 45 minutes.
2. Divide the mix between plates and serve.

Nutrition Info:

- calories 273, fat 15, fiber 11.6, carbs 16.9, protein 18.8

Beef-stuffed Baked Potatoes

Serves: 1 Potato
Cooking Time:25 Minutes

Ingredients:

- 1 lb. ground beef
- 1 large white onion, finely chopped
- 4 TB. extra-virgin olive oil
- 1 TB. seven spices
- 2 tsp. salt
- 6 large potatoes, peeled
- 1 (16-oz.) can plain tomato sauce
- 1 TB. fresh thyme
- 1 tsp. dried oregano
- 1 tsp. ground black pepper
- 1/2 tsp. garlic powder

Directions:

1. In a large skillet over medium heat, brown beef for 5 minutes, breaking up chunks with a wooden spoon.
2. Add white onion, 2 tablespoons extra-virgin olive oil, seven spices, and 1 teaspoon salt, and cook for 5 minutes.
3. Preheat the oven to 450ºF.
4. Trim bottoms of potatoes so they'll stand on end. Cut off the top 1/4 of potatoes, and set aside. Core out inside of potatoes and set aside to use in another recipe.
5. Stand potatoes inside a large casserole dish. Fill each potato with 3 tablespoons meat mixture, and place potato tops back on potatoes. Evenly drizzle potatoes with remaining 2 tablespoons extra-virgin olive oil, and bake for 15 minutes.
6. Meanwhile, in a 2-quart pot over medium heat, combine tomato sauce, remaining 1 teaspoon salt, thyme, oregano, black pepper, and garlic powder. Simmer for 10 minutes.
7. After potatoes have baked for 15 minutes, pour sauce mixture in the casserole dish around potatoes, and bake for 10 minutes.
8. Serve warm.

Beef And Grape Sauce

Servings:4
Cooking Time: 25 Minutes

Ingredients:
- 1-pound beef sirloin
- 1 teaspoon molasses
- 1 tablespoon lemon zest, grated
- 1 teaspoon soy sauce
- 1 chili pepper, chopped
- ¼ teaspoon fresh ginger, minced
- 1 cup grape juice
- ½ teaspoon salt
- 1 tablespoon butter

Directions:
1. Sprinkle the beef sirloin with salt and minced ginger.
2. Heat up butter in the saucepan and add meat.
3. Roast it for 5 minutes from each side over the medium heat.
4. After this, add soy sauce, chili pepper, and grape juice.
5. Then add lemon zest and simmer the meat for 10 minutes.
6. Add molasses and mix up meat well.
7. Close the lid and cook meat for 5 minutes.
8. Serve the cooked beef with grape juice sauce.

Nutrition Info:
- Per Servingcalories 267, fat 10, fiber 0.2, carbs 7.4, protein 34.9

Pork And Sage Couscous

Servings: 4
Cooking Time: 7 Hours

Ingredients:
- 2 pounds pork loin boneless and sliced
- ¾ cup veggie stock
- 2 tablespoons olive oil
- ½ tablespoon chili powder
- 2 teaspoon sage, dried
- ½ tablespoon garlic powder
- Salt and black pepper to the taste
- 2 cups couscous, cooked

Directions:
1. In a slow cooker, combine the pork with the stock, the oil and the other ingredients except the couscous, put the lid on and cook on Low for 7 hours.
2. Divide the mix between plates, add the couscous on the side, sprinkle the sage on top and serve.

Nutrition Info:
- calories 272, fat 14.5, fiber 9.1, carbs 16.3, protein 14.3

Tomato And Beef Casserole

Serves: 1/6 Of Casserole
Cooking Time:55 Minutes

Ingredients:
- 1/2 medium yellow onion, chopped
- 1 lb. ground beef
- 2 tsp. salt
- 1 tsp. ground black pepper
- 8 small red potatoes, washed and scrubbed
- 3 TB. extra-virgin olive oil
- 1 (16-oz.) can plain tomato sauce
- 1 cup water
- 1/2 tsp. garlic powder
- 1/2 tsp. dried oregano

Directions:
1. Preheat the oven to 450ºF.
2. In a food processor fitted with a chopping blade, blend yellow onion for 30 seconds.
3. In a large bowl, combine onions, beef, 1 teaspoon salt, and 1/2 teaspoon black pepper.
4. Spread beef mixture in an even layer in the bottom of a deep, 8×8-inch casserole dish. Bake for 20 minutes.
5. Slice red potatoes into 1/4-inch slices, and place in a bowl. Drizzle extra-virgin olive oil over top, and toss to coat. Evenly spread out potatoes on a baking sheet, and bake for 20 minutes.
6. In a medium saucepan over low heat, combine tomato sauce, water, remaining 1 teaspoon salt, remaining 1/2 teaspoon black pepper, garlic powder, and oregano. Cook for 10 minutes.
7. Remove casserole and potatoes from the oven, and using a spatula, spoon potatoes over beef. Pour tomato sauce over beef and potatoes, and bake for 15 minutes.
8. Serve warm with brown rice.

Lamb And Cauliflower Mix

Servings: 4
Cooking Time: 1 Hour

Ingredients:
- 2 pounds lamb meat, roughly cubed
- 2 tablespoons olive oil
- 1 teaspoon garlic, minced
- 1 yellow onion, chopped
- 1 teaspoon rosemary, chopped
- 1 cup veggie stock
- 2 cups cauliflower florets
- 2 tablespoons sweet paprika
- Salt and pepper to the taste

Directions:
1. Heat up a pot with the oil over medium-high heat, add the onion and the garlic and sauté for 5 minutes.
2. Add the meat and brown for 5-6 minutes more.
3. Add the rest of the ingredients, bring to a simmer and cook over medium heat for 50 minutes.
4. Divide the mix between plates and serve away.

Nutrition Info:
- calories 336, fat 14.4, fiber 10.8, carbs 21.7, protein 23.2

Lemon Leg Of Lamb Mix

Servings: 4
Cooking Time: 40 Minutes

Ingredients:
- 3 pound leg of lamb, boneless
- 2 cups goat cheese, crumbled
- 2 garlic cloves, minced
- 2 teaspoons lemon zest, grated
- 1 tablespoon olive oil
- ½ teaspoon thyme, chopped
- 1 bunch watercress
- 1 tablespoon lemon juice

Directions:
1. Grease a roasting pan with the oil, add the leg of lamb, also add the rest of the ingredients except the goat cheese, introduce in the oven and bake at 425 degrees F for 30 minutes.
2. Add the cheese, toss, bake for 10 minutes more, cool down, slice and serve.

Nutrition Info:
- calories 680, fat 55, fiber 1, carbs 4, protein 43

Cherry Stuffed Lamb

Servings:2
Cooking Time: 40 Minutes

Ingredients:
- 9 oz lamb loin
- 1 oz pistachio, chopped
- 1 teaspoon cherries, pitted
- ½ teaspoon olive oil
- ¼ teaspoon dried thyme
- 1 teaspoon dried rosemary
- 1 garlic clove, minced
- ¼ teaspoon liquid honey

Directions:
1. Rub the lamb loin with dried thyme and rosemary.
2. Then make a lengthwise cut in the meat.
3. Mix up together pistachios, minced garlic, and cherries.
4. Fill the meat with this mixture and secure the cut with the toothpick.
5. Then brush the lamb loin with liquid honey and olive oil.
6. Wrap the meat in the foil and bake at 365F for 40 minutes.
7. When the meat is cooked, remove it from the foil.
8. Let the meat chill for 10 minutes and then slice it.

Nutrition Info:
- Per Servingcalories 353, fat 20.4, fiber 1.8, carbs 6, protein 36.9

Chicken In A Bowl

Servings: 2
Cooking Time: 10 Minutes

Ingredients:
- ½ cup cooked chicken, cut into strips
- 1 head of cabbage, chopped
- 1 tablespoon coconut oil
- 1 tablespoon sesame oil
- 1/3 cup coconut aminos
- 2 garlic cloves, minced
- 2 large carrots, cut into strips
- 4 green onions, diced

Directions:
1. Melt coconut oil in a skillet over medium high heat.
2. Sauté the cabbage then add the carrots. Continue sautéing until soft. If it gets too dry, add a little bit of water.
3. Season with sesame oil and coconut aminos.
4. Add the garlic and cook for five minutes.
5. Throw in the chicken strips and toss the green onions.

Nutrition Info:
- Calories per Serving: 373.7; Carbs: 25.1g; Protein: 10.5g; Fat: 25.7g

Mustard Chops With Apricot-basil Relish

Servings: 4
Cooking Time: 12 Minutes

Ingredients:

- ¼ cup basil, finely shredded
- ¼ cup olive oil
- ½ cup mustard
- ¾ lb. fresh apricots, stone removed, and fruit diced
- 1 shallot, diced small
- 1 tsp ground cardamom
- 3 tbsp raspberry vinegar
- 4 pork chops
- Pepper and salt

Directions:

1. Make sure that pork chops are defrosted well. Season with pepper and salt. Slather both sides of each pork chop with mustard. Preheat grill to medium-high fire.
2. In a medium bowl, mix cardamom, olive oil, vinegar, basil, shallot, and apricots. Toss to combine and season with pepper and salt, mixing once again.
3. Grill chops for 5 to 6 minutes per side. As you flip, baste with mustard.
4. Serve pork chops with the Apricot-Basil relish and enjoy.

Nutrition Info:

- Calories per Serving: 486.5; Carbs: 7.3g; Protein: 42.1g; Fat: 32.1g

Lamb And Green Onions Mix

Servings: 4
Cooking Time: 25 Minutes

Ingredients:

- 1 and ½ pounds lamb, cubed
- 2 garlic cloves, minced
- 2 tablespoons olive oil
- Salt and black pepper to the taste
- ½ cup veggie stock
- ½ teaspoon saffron powder
- ¼ teaspoon cumin, ground
- 4 green onions, sliced

Directions:

1. Heat up a pan with the oil over medium-high heat, add the garlic, green onions, saffron and cumin, stir and sauté for 5 minutes.
2. Add the meat and brown it for 5 minutes more.
3. Add salt, pepper and the stock, toss, bring to a simmer and cook over medium heat for 15 minutes more.
4. Divide everything between plates and serve right away.

Nutrition Info:

- calories 292, fat 13.2, fiber 9.6, carbs 13.3, protein 14.2

Pepper Steak Taco

Servings: 4
Cooking Time: 20 Minutes

Ingredients:

- ¼ cup grated low fat Monterey Jack
- ½ avocado, sliced
- ½ cup fresh frozen corn kernels
- ½ red onion, sliced
- ½ tsp mild chili powder
- 1 lb. flank or hanger steak
- 1 tsp salt
- 2 garlic cloves, crushed
- 2 tbsp chopped fresh cilantro
- 2 tbsp sliced pickled jalapenos
- 3 bell pepper, 1 each red, yellow and orange, sliced thinly
- 3 tsp vegetable oil
- 8 small corn tortillas, warmed
- Juice of 1 lime, plus lime wedges for serving

Directions:

1. In a re-sealable plastic bag, mix chili powder, garlic, salt and lime juice until salt is dissolved. Add steak and marinate for at least 30 minutes while making sure to flip over or toss around steak halfway through the marinating time.
2. On high fire, place a large saucepan and heat 2 tsp oil. Once hot, sauté bell peppers and red onion for 5 minutes. Add corn and continue sautéing for another 3 to 5 minutes. Transfer veggies to a bowl and keep warm.
3. With paper towel, wipe skillet and return to medium high fire. Heat remaining teaspoon of oil. Once hot add steak in pan in a single layer and cook 4 minutes per side for medium rare. Remove from fire and let it rest for 5minutes on a chopping board before cutting into thin slices.
4. To make tortilla, layer jalapenos, cilantro, Monterey Jack, avocado, steak and veggies. Best serve with a dollop of sour cream.

Nutrition Info:

- Calories per Serving: 419.7; Carbs: 36.2g; Protein: 31.6g; Fat: 16.5g

Garlic Lamb And Peppers

Servings: 4
Cooking Time: 1 Hour And 30 Minutes

Ingredients:

- 1 red bell pepper, sliced
- 1 green bell pepper, sliced
- 1 yellow bell pepper, sliced
- 2 tablespoons olive oil
- 1/3 cup mint, chopped
- 4 garlic cloves, minced
- ½ cup veggie stock
- 1 and ½ tablespoon lemon juice
- 4 lamb chops
- Salt and black pepper to the taste

Directions:

1. Heat up a pan with the oil over medium-high heat, add the lamb chops and brown for 4 minutes on each side.
2. Add the rest of the ingredients, introduce the pan in the oven and bake at 370 degrees F for 1 hour and 20 minutes.
3. Divide the mix between plates and serve.

Nutrition Info:

- calories 300, fat 14.1, fiber 9.4, carbs 15.7, protein 24.2

Square Meat Pies (sfeeha)

Serves: 1 Meat Pie
Cooking Time:20 Minutes

Ingredients:

- 1 large yellow onion
- 2 large tomatoes
- 1 lb. ground beef
- 11/4 tsp. salt
- 1/2 tsp. ground black pepper
- 1 tsp. seven spices
- 1 batch Multipurpose Dough (recipe in Chapter 12)

Directions:

1. Preheat the oven to 425ºF.
2. In a food processor fitted with a chopping blade, pulse yellow onion and tomatoes for 30 seconds.
3. Transfer tomato-onion mixture to a large bowl. Add beef, salt, black pepper, and seven spices, and mix well.
4. Form Multipurpose Dough into 18 balls, and roll out to 4-inch circles. Spoon 2 tablespoons meat mixture onto center of each dough circle. Pinch together the two opposite sides of dough up to meat mixture, and pinch the opposite two sides together, forming a square. Place meat pies on a baking sheet, and bake for 20 minutes.
5. Serve warm or at room temperature.

Lamb And Peanuts Mix

Servings: 4
Cooking Time: 20 Minutes

Ingredients:

- 2 tablespoons lime juice
- 1 tablespoon balsamic vinegar
- 5 garlic cloves, minced
- 2 tablespoons olive oil
- Salt and black pepper to the taste
- 1 and ½ pound lamb meat, cubed
- 3 tablespoons peanuts, toasted and chopped
- 2 scallions, chopped

Directions:

1. Heat up a pan with the oil over medium-high heat, add the meat, and cook for 4 minutes on each side.
2. Add the scallions and the garlic and sauté for 2 minutes more.
3. Add the rest of the ingredients, toss cook for 10 minutes more, divide between plates and serve right away.

Nutrition Info:

- calories 300, fat 14.5, fiber 9.1, carbs 15.7, protein 17.5

Beef Meatballs

Servings:3
Cooking Time: 5 Minutes

Ingredients:

- ¾ teaspoon fresh ginger, minced
- 1 teaspoon dried parsley
- ¼ teaspoon ground coriander
- ½ teaspoon salt
- ¼ teaspoon chili flakes
- ¼ teaspoon ground clove
- ½ onion, minced
- 1 cup ground beef

Directions:

1. Mix up together minced ginger, dried parsley, ground coriander, salt, chili flakes, minced onion, and ground clove.
2. Then combine together ground beef and ginger mixture.
3. When the meat mixture is homogenous, make the small balls (koftas). Press them gently.
4. Grill the beef koftas for 2 minutes from each side at 395F.

Nutrition Info:

- Per Servingcalories 96, fat 5.5, fiber 0.5, carbs 2.2, protein 9

Bean Beef Chili

Servings: 4
Cooking Time: 40 Minutes

Ingredients:
- 1 lb ground beef
- 1/2 onion, diced
- 1/2 jalapeno pepper, minced
- 1 tsp chili powder
- 1/2 bell pepper, chopped
- 1 tsp garlic, chopped
- 1 cup chicken broth
- 14 oz can black beans, rinsed and drained
- 14 oz can red beans, rinsed and drained
- Pepper
- Salt

Directions:
1. Set instant pot on sauté mode.
2. Add meat and sauté until brown.
3. Add remaining ingredients and stir well.
4. Seal pot with lid and cook on high for 35 minutes.
5. Once done, release pressure using quick release. Remove lid.
6. Stir well and serve.

Nutrition Info:
- Calories 409 Fat 8.3 g Carbohydrates 36.3 g Sugar 4.2 g Protein 46.6 g Cholesterol 101 mg

Beef And Celery Stew

Servings:2
Cooking Time: 40 Minutes

Ingredients:
- ½ cup red kidney beans, drained
- 4 oz beef sirloin, chopped
- 1 teaspoon tomato paste
- 1 oz celery stalk, chopped
- 1 white onion, chopped
- 1 tomato, chopped
- 2 cups of water
- 1 teaspoon sunflower oil
- 1 teaspoon cayenne pepper
- ½ teaspoon salt
- 1 thyme sprig

Directions:
1. Roast the beef sirloin with sunflower oil, cayenne pepper, and salt for 5 minutes. Stir it with the help of spatula from time to time.
2. After this, add celery stalk, onion, tomato, thyme sprig, and tomato paste.
3. Mix up the mixture well and add water.
4. Then add red kidney beans and close the lid.
5. Cook the stew for 35 minutes over the medium heat.

Nutrition Info:
- Per Servingcalories 316, fat 6.7, fiber 9.1, carbs 36, protein 28.8

La Paz Batchoy (beef Noodle Soup La Paz Style)

Servings: 4
Cooking Time: 25 Minutes

Ingredients:
- 4 cups zucchini, spiral
- 1 cup carrots, spiral
- 1 cup jicama, spiral
- 2 pcs Beef Knorr Cubes
- 8 cups water
- 2 tbsp fish sauce
- freshly ground pepper to taste
- 3 stalks green onions, chopped
- ¼ lb beef, thinly sliced
- 4 tbsp ground pork rinds (chicharon), divided
- 2 hardboiled eggs, halved

Directions:
1. In a pot, bring water to a boil. Add Knorr cubes and fish sauce.
2. With a strainer, dip into the boiling water the zucchini noodles and cook for 3 minutes. Remove from water, drain and arrange into 4 bowls. If needed, you can cook zucchini noodles in batches.
3. Next, cook the carrots in the boiling pot of water using a strainer still. Around 2-3 minutes, drain and arrange on top of the zucchini noodles.
4. Do the same with jicama, cook in the pot, drain and arrange equally into the bowls.
5. Do the same for the thinly sliced beef. Cook for 5-10 minutes in the boiling pot of soup, swirling the strainer occasionally to ensure uniform cooking for the beef. Arrange equally on the 4 bowls.
6. Sprinkle 1 tbsp of ground pork rinds on each bowl, topped by chopped green onions, ½ hardboiled egg and freshly ground pepper.
7. Taste the boiling pot of soup and adjust to your taste. It should be slightly saltier than the usual so that the noodles will absorb the excess salt once you pour it into the bowls. Add more fish sauce to make it salty or add water to make the pot less salty. Keep soup on a rolling boil before pouring 1-2 cups of soup on each bowl. Serve right away.

Nutrition Info:
- Calories per serving: 106; Carbs: 7.8g; Protein: 10.4g; Fat: 4.0g

Chicken Burgers With Brussel Sprouts Slaw

Servings: 4
Cooking Time: 15 Minutes

Ingredients:

- ¼ cup apple, diced
- ¼ cup green onion, diced
- ½ avocado, cubed
- ½ pound Brussels sprouts, shredded
- 1 garlic clove, minced
- 1 tablespoon Dijon mustard
- 1/3 cup apple, sliced into strips
- 1/8 teaspoon red pepper flakes, optional
- 1-pound cooked ground chicken
- 3 slices bacon, cooked and diced
- Salt and pepper to taste

Directions:

1. In a mixing bowl, combine together chicken, green onion, Dijon mustard, garlic, apple, bacon and pepper flakes. Season with salt and pepper to taste. Mix the ingredients then form 4 burger patties.
2. Heat a grill pan over medium-high flame and grill the burgers. Cook for five minutes on side. Set aside.
3. In another bowl, toss the Brussels sprouts and apples.
4. In a small pan, heat coconut oil and add the Brussels sprouts mixture until everything is slightly wilted. Season with salt and pepper to taste.
5. Serve burger patties with the Brussels sprouts slaw.

Nutrition Info:

- Calories per Serving: 325.1; Carbs: 11.5g; Protein: 32.2g; Fat: 16.7g

Grilled Shrimp Sandwiches With Pesto

Serves: 1 Sandwich
Cooking Time:4 Minutes

Ingredients:

- 1 lb. fresh medium shrimp (36 to 40), shells and veins removed
- 1 tsp. salt
- 11/2 tsp. ground black pepper
- 1/3 cup plus 4 TB. extra-virgin olive oil
- 4 cups fresh basil leaves
- 3 large cloves garlic
- 1/4 cup lemon juice
- 1/3 cup toasted pine nuts
- 1/3 cup grated Parmesan cheese
- 3 cups fresh arugula
- 3 TB. balsamic vinegar
- 5 slices Havarti cheese
- 5 panini rolls, split

Directions:

1. Preheat a grill to medium heat.
2. In a medium bowl, toss shrimp with 1/2 teaspoon salt, 1/2 teaspoon black pepper, and 2 tablespoons extra-virgin olive oil. Thread shrimp onto skewers, and grill for 2 minutes per side. Set aside.
3. In a food processor fitted with a chopping blade, blend basil, remaining 1/2 teaspoon salt, 1/2 teaspoon black pepper, garlic, lemon juice, pine nuts, Parmesan cheese, and 1/3 cup extra-virgin olive oil for 2 minutes, intermittently scraping down the sides of the food processor bowl with a rubber spatula.
4. In a small bowl, toss arugula with remaining 2 tablespoons extra-virgin olive oil, balsamic vinegar, and remaining 1/2 teaspoon black pepper.
5. To assemble sandwiches, spread 1 tablespoon pesto on each side of rolls, add 1/5 of shrimp, 1 slice Havarti cheese, 1/5 of arugula, and other half of rolls. Serve immediately.

Roasted Basil Pork

Servings: 6
Cooking Time: 3 Hours

Ingredients:

- 3 tablespoons garlic, minced
- 1 tablespoon sweet paprika
- 1 tablespoon basil, chopped
- 3 tablespoons olive oil
- 4 pounds pork shoulder
- Salt and black pepper to the taste

Directions:

1. In a roasting pan, combine the pork with the garlic and the other ingredients, toss and bake at 365 degrees F and bake for 3 hours.
2. Take pork shoulder out of the oven, slice, divide between plates and serve with a side salad.

Nutrition Info:

- calories 303, fat 14, fiber 14.1, carbs 20.2, protein 17.2

Other Mediterranean Recipes

Other Mediterranean Recipes

Fig And Walnut Skillet Frittata

Servings: 4
Cooking Time: 15 Minutes

Ingredients:
- 1 cup figs, halved
- 4 eggs, beaten
- 1 teaspoon cinnamon
- A pinch of salt
- 2 tablespoons almond flour
- 2 tablespoons coconut flour
- 1 cup walnut, chopped
- 2 tablespoons coconut oil
- 1 teaspoon cardamom
- 6 tablespoons raw honey

Directions:
1. In a mixing bowl, beat the eggs.
2. Add the coconut flour, almond flour, cardamom, honey, salt and cinnamon.
3. Mix well. Heat the coconut oil in a skillet over medium heat.
4. Add the egg mixture gently.
5. Add the walnuts and figs on top.
6. Cover and cook on medium low heat for about 10 minutes.
7. Serve hot with more honey on top.

Nutrition Info:
- Calories per serving: 221; Protein: 12.7g; Carbs: 5.9g; Fat: 16.3g

Leek And Potato Soup

Servings: 8
Cooking Time:1 Hour

Ingredients:
- 3 tablespoons olive oil
- 3 leeks, sliced
- 4 garlic cloves, chopped
- 6 potatoes, peeled and cubed
- 2 cups vegetable stock
- 2 cups water
- 1 thyme sprig
- 1 rosemary sprig
- Salt and pepper to taste

Directions:
1. Heat the oil in a soup pot and stir in the leeks. Cook for 15 minutes until slightly caramelized.
2. Add the garlic and cook for 2 more minutes.
3. Add the rest of the ingredients and season with salt and pepper.
4. Cook on low heat for 20 minutes then remove the herb sprigs and puree the soup with an immersion blender.
5. Serve the soup fresh.

Nutrition Info:
- Per Serving:Calories:179 Fat:5.5g Protein:3.4g Carbohydrates:30.6g

Mixed Chicken Soup

Servings: 8
Cooking Time:1 ¾ Hours

Ingredients:
- 1 whole chicken, cut into smaller pieces
- 1 sweet onion, chopped
- 2 celery stalks, sliced
- 2 carrots, sliced
- 2 red bell peppers, cored and diced
- 1 zucchini, cubed
- 2 potatoes, peeled and cubed
- 2 tomatoes, peeled and diced
- 2 cups vegetable stock
- 8 cups water
- Salt and pepper to taste
- 1 tablespoon lemon juice
- 2 tablespoons chopped parsley for serving

Directions:
1. Combine the chicken with stock and water in a pot. Add salt and pepper and cook on low heat for 40 minutes.
2. Add the rest of the ingredients and continue cooking for another 20-25 minutes.
3. When done, remove from heat and stir in the parsley.
4. Serve the soup warm and fresh.

Nutrition Info:
- Per Serving:Calories:103 Fat:1.6g Protein:7.3g Carbohydrates:15.4g

Cream Of White Bean Soup

Servings: 6
Cooking Time:40 Minutes

Ingredients:
- 2 tablespoons olive oil
- 2 garlic cloves, chopped
- 2 shallots, chopped
- 1 celery stalk, sliced
- 1 can white beans, drained
- 2 cups chicken stock
- 2 cups water

- 1 thyme sprig
- 1 tablespoon lemon juice
- Salt and pepper to taste

Directions:

1. Heat the oil in a soup pot and stir in the garlic, shallots and celery. Cook for 2 minutes until softened then add the rest of the ingredients.
2. Cook on low heat for 20 minutes.
3. When done, remove the thyme sprig and puree the soup with an immersion blender.
4. Serve the soup warm and fresh.

Nutrition Info:

- Per Serving:Calories:160 Fat:5.2g Protein:8.3g Carbohydrates:21.6g

Cucumber, Chicken And Mango Wrap

Servings: 1
Cooking Time: 20 Minutes

Ingredients:

- ½ of a medium cucumber cut lengthwise
- ½ of ripe mango
- 1 tbsp salad dressing of choice
- 1 whole wheat tortilla wrap
- 1-inch thick slice of chicken breast around 6-inch in length
- 2 tbsp oil for frying
- 2 tbsp whole wheat flour
- 2 to 4 lettuce leaves
- Salt and pepper to taste

Directions:

1. Slice a chicken breast into 1-inch strips and just cook a total of 6-inch strips. That would be like two strips of chicken. Store remaining chicken for future use.
2. Season chicken with pepper and salt. Dredge in whole wheat flour.
3. On medium fire, place a small and nonstick fry pan and heat oil. Once oil is hot, add chicken strips and fry until golden brown around 5 minutes per side.
4. While chicken is cooking, place tortilla wraps in oven and cook for 3 to 5 minutes. Then remove from oven and place on a plate.
5. Slice cucumber lengthwise, use only ½ of it and store remaining cucumber. Peel cucumber cut into quarter and remove pith. Place the two slices of cucumber on the tortilla wrap, 1-inch away from the edge.
6. Slice mango and store the other half with seed. Peel the mango without seed, slice into strips and place on top of the cucumber on the tortilla wrap.
7. Once chicken is cooked, place chicken beside the cucumber in a line.
8. Add cucumber leaf, drizzle with salad dressing of choice.

9. Roll the tortilla wrap, serve and enjoy.

Nutrition Info:

- Calories per Serving: 434; Fat: 10g; Protein: 21g; Carbohydrates: 65g

Spinach, Mushroom And Sausage Frittata

Servings: 4
Cooking Time: 30 Minutes

Ingredients:

- Salt and pepper to taste
- 10 eggs
- ½ small onion, chopped
- 1 cup mushroom, sliced
- 1 cup fresh spinach, chopped
- ½ pound sausage, ground
- 2 tablespoon coconut oil

Directions:

1. Preheat the oven to 3500F.
2. Heat a skillet over medium high flame and add the coconut oil.
3. Sauté the onions until softened. Add in the sausage and cook for two minutes
4. Add in the spinach and mushroom. Stir constantly until the spinach has wilted.
5. Turn off the stove and distribute the vegetable mixture evenly.
6. Pour in the beaten eggs and transfer to the oven.
7. Cook for twenty minutes or until the eggs are completely cooked through.

Nutrition Info:

- Calories per serving: 383; Protein: 24.9g; Carbs: 8.6g; Fat: 27.6g

Eggplant Stew

Serves: 1 Cup
Cooking Time:35 Minutes

Ingredients:

- 3 TB. extra-virgin olive oil
- 1 medium white onion, chopped
- 2 large carrots, sliced diagonally
- 4 medium Italian eggplant, trimmed and diced
- 2 large potatoes, peeled and diced
- 1 large tomato, diced
- 1 (16-oz.) can tomato sauce
- 1 tsp. garlic powder
- 1 tsp. paprika
- 11/2 tsp. salt
- 1 cup fresh cilantro, chopped

Directions:

1. In a 3-quart pot over medium heat, heat extra-virgin

olive oil. Add white onion and carrots, and cook for 5 minutes.

2. Add Italian eggplant and potatoes, and cook for 7 minutes.

3. Add tomato, and cook for 3 minutes.

4. Add tomato sauce, garlic powder, paprika, and salt, and simmer, stirring occasionally, for 15 minutes.

5. Stir in cilantro, and cook for 5 more minutes.

6. Serve with brown rice.

Simple And Easy Hummus

Servings: 4-5
Cooking Time: 5 Minutes

Ingredients:
• 1 can (15 ounce) chickpeas, drained and then rinsed
• 2 garlic cloves
• 3 tablespoons tahini
• 3 tablespoons olive oil
• 2 tablespoons lemon juice
• 1/2 teaspoon salt

Directions:
1. Put all the ingredients in a food processor or a blender; process or blend until the texture is pasty.

Nutrition Info:
• per serving:548 cal., 23 g total fat (3.1 g sat. fat), 0 mg chol., 331 mg sodium, 992 mg pot., 67.5 g total carbs., 19.6 g fiber, 11.6 g sugar, 22.6 g protein, 2% vitamin A, 14% vitamin C, 16% calcium, and 43% iron.

Greek Salad And Mediterranean Vinaigrette

Servings: 2-4
Cooking Time:15 Minutes

Ingredients:
• 4 Persian cucumbers, sliced into rounds (or 1 English cucumber)
• 4 campari tomatoes, cut into wedges
• 2 tablespoons Vinaigrette
• 2 ounces feta cheese, crumbled
• 1/8 cup Kalamata olives
• 1/4 small red onion, thinly sliced
• 1 tablespoon capers

Directions:
1. Except for the vinaigrette, put all of the ingredients into a large-sized salad bowl. Drizzle with the vinaigrette; toss to evenly coat. Serve.

Nutrition Info:
• Per Serving:148 cal.,8.1 g total fat (3.1 g sat. fat), 13 mg chol., 271 mg sodium, 751 mg pot., 17.3 g total carbs., 3.3 g fiber, 9.2 g sugar, 5.2 g protein,28% vitamin A, 43% vitamin C, 14% calcium, and 8% iron

Middle Eastern Spicy Chicken Wings

Servings:25
Cooking Time:45 Minutes

Ingredients:
• 2 pounds (25 pieces) large chicken wings
• 1/4 teaspoon pepper
• 1/4 cup extra-virgin olive oil
• 1/2 teaspoon allspice
• 1 teaspoon salt, plus more to taste
• 1 teaspoon paprika
• 1 teaspoon cayenne pepper (1/2 teaspoon for mild, 3/4 teaspoon for medium, 1 teaspoon for spicy, 1 1/4 teaspoon for fiery)
• 1 1/2 cups tahini sauce, recipe follows
• 2 teaspoon cumin
• 3/4 teaspoon turmeric

Directions:
1. Trim the chicken wing tips off and then with a sharp kitchen scissor, separate the wing from the drumstick; reserve the tips for later use in making chicken stock or you can discard them. When the wings and drumsticks are separated, trim off any fat or excess skin flaps.

2. In a small-sized bowl, whisk the olive oil with the spices, salt, and pepper; adjust the cayenne pepper to your taste.

3. Put the chicken drumsticks and wings in a large-sized re-sealable plastic bag or marinating dish. Pour the marinade over the chicken pieces; massage or stir to evenly coat with the marinade and put in the fridge to marinate for at least 6 hours up to 24 hours.

4. About 10 minutes before cooking, take the marinated chicken pieces out from the fridge so the marinade can soften for a little bit.

5. Preheat the oven to 400F.

6. Grease baking sheets with nonstick cooking oil; the number of baking sheets needed will depend on how big your wings are. For easier clean up, line the baking sheets with foil, if desired.

7. After 20 minutes, massage or stir the chicken to make sure the pieces are evenly coated with the spice and there are no clumps. Put the chicken in the baking sheets, spacing them evenly. Put the sheets in the oven; roast for about 45 minutes until cooked through, turning once halfway through baking using tongs.

8. If desired, season with salt to taste. Serve these spicy wings hot baked and with tahini sauce.

Nutrition Info:
• Per Serving:173 cal., 12.5 g total fat (2.1 g sat. fat), 32 mg chol., 141 mg sodium, 157 mg pot., 3.3 g total carbs., 1.4 g fiber, 0 g sugar, 13 g protein, 2% vitamin A, 0% vitamin C, 7% calcium, and 11% iron.

Veal Shank Barley Soup

Servings: 10
Cooking Time:1 ¼ Hours

Ingredients:

- 3 tablespoons olive oil
- 4 veal shanks, sliced
- 4 cups vegetable stock
- 4 cups water
- 1 sweet onion, chopped
- 2 red bell peppers, cored and diced
- 2 carrots, diced
- 2 celery stalk, sliced
- 2 tomatoes, peeled and diced
- 1 parsnip, diced
- ½ cup barley pearls, rinsed
- Salt and pepper to taste
- Chopped parsley for serving

Directions:

1. Heat the oil in a soup pot and stir in the veal shank slices. Cook for 10 minutes then add the stock and water.
2. Cook for 10 minutes then stir in the rest of the ingredients, except the parsley.
3. Continue cooking for 30 more minutes on low heat, seasoning with salt and pepper.
4. Serve the soup warm, topped with parsley.

Nutrition Info:

- Per Serving:Calories:254 Fat:9.3g Protein:26.5g Carbohydrates:15.3g

Dill, Havarti & Asparagus Frittata

Servings: 4
Cooking Time: 20 Minutes

Ingredients:

- 1 tsp dried dill weed or 2 tsp minced fresh dill
- 4-oz Havarti cheese cut into small cubes
- 6 eggs, beaten well
- Pepper and salt to taste
- 1 stalk green onions sliced for garnish
- 3 tsp. olive oil
- 2/3 cup diced cherry tomatoes
- 6-8 oz fresh asparagus, ends trimmed and cut into 1 ½-inch lengths

Directions:

1. On medium-high the fire, place a large cast-iron pan and add oil. Once oil is hot, stir-fry asparagus for 4 minutes.
2. Add dill weed and tomatoes. Cook for two minutes.
3. Meanwhile, season eggs with pepper and salt. Beat well.
4. Pour eggs over the tomatoes.
5. Evenly spread cheese on top.
6. Preheat broiler.
7. Lower the fire to low, cover pan, and let it cook for 10 minutes until the cheese on top has melted.
8. Turn off the fire and transfer pan in the oven and broil for 2 minutes or until tops are browned.
9. Remove from the oven, sprinkle sliced green onions, serve, and enjoy.

Nutrition Info:

- Calories per serving: 244; Protein: 16.0g; Carbs: 3.7g; Fat: 18.3g

Creamy Parsnip Soup

Servings: 6
Cooking Time:1 Hour

Ingredients:

- 3 tablespoons olive oil
- 2 sweet onions, chopped
- 2 leeks, sliced
- 4 parsnips, peeled and diced
- 1 celery stalk, sliced
- 1 green apple, peeled and diced
- 2 cups vegetable stock
- 2 cups water
- Salt and pepper to taste
- ¼ cup heavy cream

Directions:

1. Heat the oil in a soup pot and stir in the onions, leeks, parsnips, celery and apples, as well as stock and water.
2. Season with salt and pepper and cook for 20 minutes.
3. When done, add the cream and puree the soup with an immersion blender.
4. Serve the soup fresh.

Nutrition Info:

- Per Serving:Calories:195 Fat:2.2g Protein:2.2g Carbohydrates:28.3g

Bacon & Hot Dogs Omelet

Servings: 4
Cooking Time: 15 Minutes

Ingredients:

- 4 hot dogs, chopped
- 8 eggs
- 2 bacon slices, chopped
- 4 small onions, chopped

Directions:

1. Preheat the Airfryer to 325 degrees F.
2. Crack the eggs in an Airfryer baking pan and beat well.
3. Stir in the remaining ingredients and cook for about 10 minutes until completely done.

Nutrition Info:

- Calories: 298 Carbs: 9g Fats: 21.8g Proteins: 16.9g Sodium: 628mg Sugar: 5.1g

5-layer Mediterranean Dip

Servings: 8-12
Cooking Time: 15-30 Minutes

Ingredients:
- 8 ounces marinated artichoke hearts, chopped
- 8 ounces hummus
- 8 ounces crumbled feta cheese
- 1/2 cup chopped roasted red peppers
- 1 lemon
- 1 bag of pita chips, for serving
- 1 cup Greek yogurt
- 10 ounces frozen spinach (thawed, excess water squeezed out, and chopped)
- 2 tablespoons olive oil
- 2 tablespoons lemon juice
- Kosher salt, or to taste
- Freshly ground black pepper, or to taste
- 1 cup green olives, pitted
- 2 cloves garlic, peeled
- 1 lemon, zest only
- 2 tablespoons lemon juice
- 1/4 cup olive oil
- 1 teaspoon thyme leaves
- Kosher salt, or to taste
- Freshly ground black pepper, or to taste

Directions:
1. Put the green olive ingredients for processing into the food processor; pulse until the chopped, but still chunky. Transfer into a bowl; set aside.
2. In a medium-sized bowl, combine the spinach, 2 tablespoons olive oil, Greek yogurt, and 2 tablespoons juice of lemon; season with the salt and the pepper and set aside.
3. To assemble the layer:
4. In a serving dish, preferably glass, layer the hummus evenly in the bottom. Layer the feta cheese, artichokes, yogurt-spinach mix, green olive mix, and then with the roasted peppers.

Nutrition Info:
- Per Serving:283 cal., 21.4 g total fat (6.9 g sat. fat), 27 mg chol., 666 mg sodium, 484 mg pot., 14.2 g total carbs., 5.1 g fiber, 4 g sugar, 12.3 g protein, 77% vitamin A, 71% vitamin C, 26% calcium, and 17% iron.

Tahini Yogurt Sauce

Servings:3/4
Cooking Time: 5 Minutes

Ingredients:
- 6 tablespoons Greek yogurt
- 2 tablespoons tahini paste
- 2 tablespoons freshly squeezed lemon juice
- 1/4 teaspoon salt
- 1 garlic clove, pressed

Directions:
1. In a medium bowl, mix all the ingredients until well blended; serve as accompaniment to suggested dish.

Nutrition Info:
- per serving: 271 cal., 18.5 g total fat (4.1 g sat. fat), 5 mg chol., 657 mg sodium, 325 mg pot., 12.3 g total carbs., 3 g fiber, 5.1 g sugar, 16.3 g protein, 1% vitamin A, 25% vitamin C, 24% calcium, and 15% iron.

Coconut Flour Pizza

Servings: 4
Cooking Time: 35 Minutes

Ingredients:
- 2 tablespoons psyllium husk powder
- ¾ cup coconut flour
- 1 teaspoon garlic powder
- ½ teaspoon salt
- ½ teaspoon baking soda
- 1 cup boiling water
- 1 teaspoon apple cider vinegar
- 3 eggs
- Toppings
- 3 tablespoons tomato sauce
- 1½ oz. Mozzarella cheese
- 1 tablespoon basil, freshly chopped

Directions:
1. Preheat the oven to 350 degrees F and grease a baking sheet.
2. Mix coconut flour, salt, psyllium husk powder, and garlic powder until fully combined.
3. Add eggs, apple cider vinegar, and baking soda and knead with boiling water.
4. Place the dough out on a baking sheet and top with the toppings.
5. Transfer in the oven and bake for about 20 minutes.
6. Dish out and serve warm.

Nutrition Info:
- Calories: 173 Carbs: 16.8g Fats: 7.4g Proteins: 10.4g Sodium: 622mg Sugar: 0.9g

Mediterranean Sunset

Servings:1
Cooking Time:2 Minutes

Ingredients:
- 1 ounce ouzo, or more to taste
- 1 tablespoon grenadine
- Orange juice or lemonade or grapefruit juice

Directions:
1. Fill a highball glass with ice cubes. Add all of the ingredients into a shaker; shake to mix. Pour the concoction into the highball glass. Enjoy!

Nutrition Info:
- Per Serving:47 cal., 0 g total fat (0 g sat. fat), 0 mg chol., 1170 mg sodium, 7 mg pot., 12.4 g total carbs., 0 g fiber, 12.3 g sugar, 0 g protein, 0% vitamin A, 5% vitamin C, 0% calcium, and 0% iron.

Arrabbiata White Bean Soup

Servings: 8
Cooking Time:1 Hour

Ingredients:
- 2 tablespoons olive oil
- 2 carrots, diced
- 1 sweet onion, chopped
- 2 garlic cloves, chopped
- ½ teaspoon chili flakes
- 1 can diced tomatoes
- 1 can white beans, drained
- 4 cups chicken stock
- 4 cups water
- 1 bay leaf
- Salt and pepper to taste

Directions:
1. Heat the oil in a soup pot and stir in the carrots, onion, garlic and chili flakes.
2. Cook for 5 minutes then add the tomatoes, beans, stock, water and bay leaf, as well as salt and pepper.
3. Cook on low heat for 25 minutes.
4. Serve the soup warm and fresh.

Nutrition Info:
- Per Serving:Calories:135 Fat:4.0g Protein:6.7g Carbohydrates:19.3g

Paleo Almond Banana Pancakes

Servings: 3
Cooking Time: 10 Minutes

Ingredients:
- ¼ cup almond flour
- ½ teaspoon ground cinnamon
- 3 eggs
- 1 banana, mashed
- 1 tablespoon almond butter
- 1 teaspoon vanilla extract
- 1 teaspoon olive oil
- Sliced banana to serve

Directions:
1. Whisk the eggs in a mixing bowl until they become fluffy.
2. In another bowl mash the banana using a fork and add to the egg mixture.
3. Add the vanilla, almond butter, cinnamon and almond flour.
4. Mix into a smooth batter.
5. Heat the olive oil in a skillet.
6. Add one spoonful of the batter and fry them from both sides.
7. Keep doing these steps until you are done with all the batter.
8. Add some sliced banana on top before serving.

Nutrition Info:
- Calories per serving: 306; Protein: 14.4g; Carbs: 3.6g; Fat: 26.0g

Tuscan Cabbage Soup

Servings: 8
Cooking Time:1 Hour

Ingredients:
- 2 tablespoons olive oil
- 2 sweet onions, chopped
- 2 carrots, grated
- 1 celery stalk, chopped
- 1 can diced tomatoes
- 1 cabbage, shredded
- 2 cups vegetable stock
- 2 cups water
- 1 lemon, juiced
- 1 thyme sprig
- 1 oregano sprig
- 1 basil sprig
- Salt and pepper to taste

Directions:
1. Heat the oil in a soup pot and stir in the onions, carrots and celery.
2. Cook for 5 minutes then stir in the rest of the ingredients.
3. Season with salt and pepper to taste and cook on low heat for 25 minutes.
4. Serve the soup warm.

Nutrition Info:
- Per Serving:Calories:58 Fat:3.6g Protein:1.0g Carbohydrates:6.6g

St. Valentine's Mediterranean Pancakes

Servings: 2
Cooking Time:20 Minutes

Ingredients:
- 4 eggs, preferably organic
- 2 pieces banana, peeled and then cut into small pieces
- 1/2 teaspoon extra-virgin olive oil (for the pancake pan)
- 1 tablespoon milled flax seeds, preferably organic
- 1 tablespoon bee pollen, milled, preferably organic

Directions:
1. Crack the eggs into a mixing bowl. Add in the banana, flax seeds, and bee pollen. With a hand mixer, blend the ingredients until smooth batter inn texture.
2. Put a few drops of the olive oil in a nonstick pancake pan over medium flame or heat. Pour some batter into the pan; cook for about 2 minutes, undisturbed until the bottom of the pancake is golden and can be lifted easily from the pan. With a silicon spatula, lift and flip the pancake; cook for about 30seconds more and transfer into a plate.
3. Repeat the process with the remaining batter, oiling the pan with every new batter.
4. Serve the pancake as you cook or serve them all together topped with vanilla, strawberry, pine nuts jam.

Nutrition Info:
- Per Serving:272 cal.,11.6 g total fat (3 g sat. fat), 327 mg chol., 125 mg sodium, 633 mg pot., 32.7 g total carbs., 4.5 g fiber, 17.3 g sugar, 13.3 g protein, 10% vitamin A, 20% vitamin C, 6% calcium, and 12% iron

Mushroom, Spinach And Turmeric Frittata

Servings: 6
Cooking Time: 35 Minutes

Ingredients:
- ½ tsp pepper
- ½ tsp salt
- 1 tsp turmeric
- 5-oz firm tofu
- 4 large eggs
- 6 large egg whites
- ¼ cup water
- 1 lb fresh spinach
- 6 cloves freshly chopped garlic
- 1 large onion, chopped
- 1 lb button mushrooms, sliced

Directions:
1. Grease a 10-inch nonstick and oven proof skillet and preheat oven to 350oF.
2. Place skillet on medium high fire and add mushrooms. Cook until golden brown.
3. Add onions, cook for 3 minutes or until onions are tender.
4. Add garlic, sauté for 30 seconds.
5. Add water and spinach, cook while covered until spinach is wilted, around 2 minutes.
6. Remove lid and continue cooking until water is fully evaporated.
7. In a blender, puree pepper, salt, turmeric, tofu, eggs and egg whites until smooth. Pour into skillet once liquid is fully evaporated.
8. Pop skillet into oven and bake until the center is set around 25-30 minutes.
9. Remove skillet from oven and let it stand for ten minutes before inverting and transferring to a serving plate.
10. Cut into 6 equal wedges, serve and enjoy.

Nutrition Info:
- Calories per serving: 166; Protein: 15.9g; Carbs: 12.2g; Fat: 6.0g

Dessert Recipes

Dessert Recipes

Honey Fruit Compote

Servings: 4
Cooking Time: 3 Minutes

Ingredients:
- 1/3 cup honey
- 1 1/2 cups blueberries
- 1 1/2 cups raspberries

Directions:
1. Add all ingredients into the instant pot and stir well.
2. Seal pot with lid and cook on high for 3 minutes.
3. Once done, allow to release pressure naturally. Remove lid.
4. Serve and enjoy.

Nutrition Info:
- Calories 141 Fat 0.5 g Carbohydrates 36.7 g Sugar 30.6 g Protein 1 g Cholesterol 0 mg

Mixed Berries Stew

Servings: 6
Cooking Time: 15 Minutes

Ingredients:
- Zest of 1 lemon, grated
- Juice of 1 lemon
- ½ pint blueberries
- 1 pint strawberries, halved
- 2 cups water
- 2 tablespoons stevia

Directions:
1. In a pan, combine the berries with the water, stevia and the other ingredients, bring to a simmer, cook over medium heat for 15 minutes, divide into bowls and serve cold.

Nutrition Info:
- calories 172, fat 7, fiber 3.4, carbs 8, protein 2.3

Lemon Cranberry Sauce

Servings: 8
Cooking Time: 14 Minutes

Ingredients:
- 10 oz fresh cranberries
- 3/4 cup Swerve
- 1/4 cup water
- 1 tsp lemon zest
- 1 tsp vanilla extract

Directions:
1. Add cranberries and water into the instant pot.
2. Seal pot with lid and cook on high for 1 minute.
3. Once done, allow to release pressure naturally for 10 minutes then release remaining using quick release. Remove lid.
4. Set pot on sauté mode.
5. Add remaining ingredients and cook for 2-3 minutes.
6. Pour in container and store in fridge.

Nutrition Info:
- Calories 21 Fat 0 g Carbohydrates 25.8 g Sugar 23.9 g Protein 0 g Cholesterol 0 mg

Coconut Cookies

Servings: 4
Cooking Time:45 Minutes

Ingredients:
- 3 cups shredded coconut
- 4 eggs whites
- 1 teaspoon vanilla extract
- 1 teaspoon lime zest

Directions:
1. Mix the coconut with the egg whites, vanilla and lime zest.
2. Form small balls of this mixture and place them on a baking tray lined with parchment paper.
3. Bake in the preheated oven at 330F for 20 minutes.
4. Serve the cookies chilled and store them in an airtight container.

Nutrition Info:
- Per Serving:Calories:279 Fat:24.4g Protein:7.6g Carbohydrates: 9.7g

Mediterranean Cheesecake

Servings: 8
Cooking Time:20 Minutes

Ingredients:
- 1 package (8 ounces) cream cheese
- 1/4 cup sour cream
- 1/2 cup condensed milk, sweetened
- 5 tablespoons sugar, divided
- 1 tablespoon vanilla
- 1 tablespoon orange blossom
- 1 tablespoon rose water
- 1 tablespoon orange zest
- 1 egg
- 1/2 cup butter
- 2 cups phyllo dough or kadaifi
- 1/2 cup toasted coconut
- 1/2 cup pistachios
- 1/2 cup simple syrup

Directions:
1. Preheat the oven to 325F.
2. With a hand mixer, mix the condensed milk, cream cheese, and the sour cream in a large bowl until well blended. Alternatively, you can blend them until well blended.
3. Add the orange zest, orange blossom, rose water, vanilla, and sugar, blend for 1 minute. Add in the egg and blend for 30 seconds.
4. In another bowl, break the kadaifi into pieces. Add 3 tablespoons of the sugar, and the butter, mix until well combined.
5. Line the bottom and the sides of a cheesecake pan or a muffin tin with the kadaifi mixture.
6. Pour the cheesecake mixture into the cheesecake pan or muffin tin, filling 80% of the container. Place into the oven and bake for 20 minutes. Remove from the oven and let completely cool before serving.
7. When completely cool, slice the cake into 8 portions, top with the syrup, pistachio and/or coconut, and glaze with more simple syrup. Serve.

Nutrition Info:
- Per Serving:742 cal., 43 g total fat (23 g sat. fat), 129.3 mg chol., 526.5 mg sodium, 78 g total carbs., 2.6 g fiber, 43.1 g sugar, 12 g protein, 24.8% vitamin A, 6.1% vitamin C, 14.3% calcium, and 15.4% iron.

Mediterranean Diet Cookie Recipe

Servings: 12
Cooking Time: 40 Minutes

Ingredients:
- 1 tsp vanilla extract
- ½ tsp salt
- 4 large egg whites
- 1 ¼ cups sugar
- 2 cups toasted and skinned hazelnuts

Directions:
1. Preheat oven to 325oF and position oven rack in the center. Then line with baking paper your baking pan.
2. In a food processor, finely grind the hazelnuts and then transfer into a medium sized bowl.
3. In a large mixing bowl, on high speed beat salt and egg whites until stiff and there is formation of peaks. Then gently fold in the ground nut and vanilla until thoroughly mixed.
4. Drop a spoonful of the mixture onto prepared pan and bake the cookies for twenty minutes or until lightly browned per batch. Bake 6 cookies per cookie sheet.
5. Let it cool on pan for five minutes before removing.

Nutrition Info:
- Calorie per Servings: 173; Carbs: 23.0g; Protein: 3.1g; Fats: 7.6g

Strawberry And Avocado Medley

Servings: 4
Cooking Time: 5 Minutes

Ingredients:
- 2 cups strawberry, halved
- 1 avocado, pitted and sliced
- 2 tablespoons slivered almonds

Directions:
1. Place all Ingredients: in a mixing bowl.
2. Toss to combine.
3. Allow to chill in the fridge before serving.

Nutrition Info:
- Calories per serving: 107; Carbs: 9.9g; Protein: 1.6g; Fat: 7.8g

Custard Cookie Trifle

Serves: ½ Trifle
Cooking Time:20 Minutes

Ingredients:
- 1 cup sugar
- 1/2 cup all-purpose flour
- 1/4 tsp. salt
- 3 cups whole milk
- 4 large egg yolks, beaten
- 3 TB. butter
- 1 TB. vanilla extract
- 2 cups milk chocolate chips
- 1/2 cup heavy cream
- 40 vanilla wafers

Directions:

1. In a large pot over medium heat, whisk together sugar, all-purpose flour, salt, and whole milk. Simmer for 4 minutes, continually stirring.

2. In a small bowl, whisk together egg yolks. While whisking, slowly pour 1 cup of hot milk mixture into eggs. Pour egg mixture back into the pot, continue to stir, and simmer for 2 minutes.

3. Stir in butter and vanilla extract until combined, and remove from heat.

4. Place milk chocolate chips and heavy cream in a bowl. Using a double boiler or a microwave, melt chocolate.

5. To form trifle, place a layer of vanilla wafers on the bottom of a 9×9-inch baking dish. Pour 1/2 of custard mixture over cookies, drizzle 1/2 of chocolate mixture over custard, and repeat, ending with a layer of chocolate on top.

6. Refrigerate for 2 hours before serving.

Greek Yogurt Pie

Servings: 8
Cooking Time:1 Hour

Ingredients:
- 1 package phyllo dough sheets
- 4 cups plain yogurt
- 4 eggs
- ½ cup white sugar
- 1 teaspoon vanilla extract
- 1 teaspoon lemon zest
- 1 teaspoon orange zest

Directions:

1. Mix the yogurt, eggs, sugar, vanilla and citrus zest in a bowl.

2. Layer 2 phyllo sheets in a deep dish baking pan then pour a few tablespoons of yogurt mixture over the dough.

3. Continue layering the phyllo dough and yogurt in the pan.

4. Bake in the preheated oven at 350F for 40 minutes.

5. Allow the pie to cool down before serving.

Nutrition Info:
- Per Serving:Calories:175 Fat:3.8g Protein:9.9g Carbohydrates:22.7g

Walnuts Kataifi

Servings:2
Cooking Time: 50 Minutes

Ingredients:
- 7 oz kataifi dough
- 1/3 cup walnuts, chopped
- ½ teaspoon ground cinnamon
- ¾ teaspoon vanilla extract
- 4 tablespoons butter, melted
- ¼ teaspoon ground clove
- 1/3 cup water
- 3 tablespoons honey

Directions:

1. For the filling: mix up together walnuts, ground cinnamon, and vanilla extract. Add ground clove and blend the mixture until smooth.

2. Make the kataifi dough: grease the casserole mold with butter and place ½ part of kataifi dough.

3. Then sprinkle the filling over the kataifi dough.

4. After this, sprinkle the filling with 1 tablespoon of melted butter.

5. Sprinkle the filling with remaining kataifi dough.

6. Make the roll from ½ part of kataifi dough and cut it.

7. Gently arrange the kataifi roll in the tray.

8. Repeat the same steps with remaining dough. In the end, you should get 2 kataifi rolls.

9. Preheat the oven to 355F and place the tray with kataifi rolls inside.

10. Bake the dessert for 50 minutes or until it is crispy.

11. Meanwhile, make the syrup: bring the water to boil.

12. Add honey and heat it up until the honey is dissolved.

13. When the kataifi rolls are cooked, pour the hot syrup over the hot kataifi rolls.

14. Cut every kataifi roll on 2 pieces.

15. Serve the dessert with remaining syrup.

Nutrition Info:
- Per Servingcalories 120, fat 1.5, fiber 0, carbs 22, protein 3

Blackberry Jam

Servings: 6
Cooking Time: 6 Hours

Ingredients:
- 3 cups fresh blackberries
- 1/4 cup chia seeds
- 4 tbsp Swerve
- 1/4 cup fresh lemon juice
- 1/4 cup coconut butter

Directions:
1. Add all ingredients into the instant pot and stir well.
2. Seal the pot with a lid and select slow cook mode and cook on low for 6 hours.
3. Pour in container and store in fridge.

Nutrition Info:
- Calories 101 Fat 6.8 g Carbohydrates 20 g Sugar 14.4 g Protein 2 g Cholesterol 0 mg

Cold Lemon Squares

Servings: 4
Cooking Time: 0 Minutes

Ingredients:
- 1 cup avocado oil+ a drizzle
- 2 bananas, peeled and chopped
- 1 tablespoon honey
- ¼ cup lemon juice
- A pinch of lemon zest, grated

Directions:
1. In your food processor, mix the bananas with the rest of the ingredients, pulse well and spread on the bottom of a pan greased with a drizzle of oil.
2. Introduce in the fridge for 30 minutes, slice into squares and serve.

Nutrition Info:
- calories 136, fat 11.2, fiber 0.2, carbs 7, protein 1.1

Peanut Banana Yogurt Bowl

Servings: 4
Cooking Time: 15 Minutes

Ingredients:
- 4 cups Greek yogurt
- 2 medium bananas, sliced
- ¼ cup creamy natural peanut butter
- ¼ cup flax seed meal
- 1 teaspoon nutmeg

Directions:
1. Divide the yogurt between four bowls and top with banana, peanut butter, and flax seed meal.
2. Garnish with nutmeg.
3. Chill before serving.

Nutrition Info:
- Calories per serving: 370; Carbs: 47.7g; Protein: 22.7g; Fat: 10.6g

Strawberry Banana Greek Yogurt Parfaits

Servings: 4
Cooking Time: 5 Minutes

Ingredients:
- 1 cup plain Greek yogurt, chilled
- 1 cup pepitas
- ½ cup chopped strawberries
- ½ banana, sliced

Directions:
1. In a parfait glass, add the yogurt at the bottom of the glass.
2. Add a layer of pepitas, strawberries, and bananas.
3. Continue to layer the Ingredients: until the entire glass is filled.

Nutrition Info:
- Calories per serving:387; Carbs: 69.6g; Protein: 18.1g; Fat: 1g

Strawberry Ice Cream

Servings: 6
Cooking Time:1 ¼ Hours

Ingredients:
- 1 pound strawberries, hulled
- 1 cup Greek yogurt
- 1 cup heavy cream
- 3 tablespoons honey
- 1 teaspoon lime zest

Directions:
1. Combine all the ingredients in a blender and pulse until well mixed and smooth.
2. Pour the mixture into your ice cream machine and churn for 1 hour or according to your machine's instructions.
3. Serve the ice cream right away.

Nutrition Info:
- Per Serving:Calories:150 Fat:8.3g Protein:4.3g Carbohydrates:16.4g

Spiced Walnut Cake

Servings: 8
Cooking Time:1 Hour

Ingredients:
- ¼ cup hot water
- ½ pound dates, pitted
- 2 cups walnuts, ground
- ½ cup light brown sugar
- 2/3 cup almond flour
- 4 eggs
- 1 teaspoon orange zest
- 1 teaspoon lemon zest
- ½ teaspoon cinnamon powder
- ¼ teaspoon ground ginger
- 1 teaspoon vanilla extract
- 1 pinch salt

Directions:
1. Combine the hot water and dates in a blender and pulse until well mixed and smooth.
2. Add the eggs, vanilla and spices and pulse well.
3. Add the sugar and mix well then fold in the ground walnuts and almond flour, as well as a pinch of salt.
4. Pour the batter in a 8-inch round cake pan lined with baking paper.
5. Bake in the preheated oven at 350F for 35-40 minutes or until it passes the toothpick test.
6. Allow the cake to cool in the pan when done.
7. Slice and serve it fresh or store in an airtight container.

Nutrition Info:
- Per Serving:Calories:341 Fat:20.7g Protein:11.0g Carbohydrates:33.7g

Almond Peaches Mix

Servings: 4
Cooking Time: 10 Minutes

Ingredients:
- 1/3 cup almonds, toasted
- 1/3 cup pistachios, toasted
- 1 teaspoon mint, chopped
- ½ cup coconut water
- 1 teaspoon lemon zest, grated
- 4 peaches, halved
- 2 tablespoons stevia

Directions:
1. In a pan, combine the peaches with the stevia and the rest of the ingredients, simmer over medium heat for 10 minutes, divide into bowls and serve cold.

Nutrition Info:
- calories 135, fat 4.1, fiber 3.8, carbs 4.1, protein 2.3

Minty Fruit Salad

Servings: 4
Cooking Time:35 Minutes

Ingredients:
- 1 cup strawberries, halved
- 1 cup white grapes, halved
- 1 mango, peeled and cubed
- 2 oranges, cut into segments
- 4 kiwi fruits, peeled and cubed
- 3 tablespoons honey
- 2 tablespoons lemon juice
- 4 mint leaves, chopped

Directions:
1. Combine the strawberries, grapes, mango, oranges and kiwi fruits in a bowl.
2. For the sauce, mix the honey, lemon juice and mint in a bowl.
3. Pour the sauce over the fruits and serve right away.

Nutrition Info:
- Per Serving:Calories:138 Fat:0.6g Protein:1.9g Carbohydrates:34.4g

Frozen Strawberry Greek Yogurt

Servings: 16
Cooking Time: 15 Minutes

Ingredients:
- 3 cups Greek yogurt, plain, low-fat (2%)
- 2 teaspoons vanilla
- 1/8 teaspoon salt
- 1/4 cup freshly squeezed lemon juice
- 1 cup sugar
- 1 cup strawberries, sliced

Directions:
1. In a medium-sized bowl, except for the strawberries, combine the rest of the ingredients; whisking until the mixture is smooth.
2. Transfer the yogurt into a 1 1/2 or 2-quart ice cream make and freeze according to the manufacturer's direction, adding the strawberry slices for the last minute. Transfer into an airtight container and freeze for about 2-4 hours. Before serving, let stand for 15 minutes at room temperature.

Nutrition Info:
- Per Serving:86 cal., 1 g total fat (1 g sat. fat), 3 mg chol., 16g carbs., 0 g fiber, 15 g sugar, and 4 g protein.

Date Cake

Serves: 1 Piece
Cooking Time:35 Minutes

Ingredients:
- 8 dates, pitted and finely chopped
- 3/4 cup water
- 1 tsp. baking soda
- 3/4 cup sugar
- 1/2 cup butter
- 2 large eggs
- 1 TB. vanilla extract
- 21/2 cups all-purpose flour
- 1/2 tsp. salt
- 1/2 tsp. cinnamon
- 2 tsp. baking powder
- 3/4 cup confectioners' sugar
- 3 TB. whole milk
- 2 TB. tahini paste

Directions:
1. Preheat the oven to 350ºF. Lightly coat a 9×13-inch cake pan or Bundt pan with cooking spray, and dust with about 2 tablespoons all-purpose flour.
2. In a medium saucepan over low heat, combine dates and water, and cook, stirring occasionally, for 5 minutes. Remove from heat.
3. Stir in baking soda, remove date mixture from the pan, and set aside to cool.
4. In a large bowl, and using an electric mixer on medium speed, blend cooled dates, sugar, butter, eggs, and vanilla extract for 2 minutes.
5. Add all-purpose flour, salt, cinnamon, and baking powder, blend for 2 more minutes.
6. Pour batter into the prepared pan, and bake for 35 minutes.
7. Cool cake completely.
8. In a small bowl, whisk together confectioners' sugar, whole milk, and tahini paste. If mixture is too thick, add another 1 tablespoon milk until it has the consistency of glaze.
9. When cake is cool, pour glaze over top, cut, and serve.

Melon Ice Cream

Servings:4
Cooking Time: 2 Hours

Ingredients:
- 9 oz melon, peeled, chopped
- 1 tablespoon Erythritol
- ½ cup of orange juice

Directions:
1. Blend the melon until smooth and combine it with Erythritol and orange juice.
2. Mix up the liquid until Erythritol is dissolved.
3. Then pour the liquid into the popsicles molds.

4. Freeze the popsicles for 2 hours in the freezer.

Nutrition Info:
- Per Servingcalories 36, fat 0.2, fiber 0.6, carbs 12.2, protein 0.8

Coconut Risotto Pudding

Servings: 6
Cooking Time: 20 Minutes

Ingredients:
- 3/4 cup rice
- 1/2 cup shredded coconut
- 1 tsp lemon juice
- 1/2 tsp vanilla
- oz can coconut milk
- 1/4 cup maple syrup
- 1 1/2 cups water

Directions:
1. Add all ingredients into the instant pot and stir well.
2. Seal pot with lid and cook on high for 20 minutes.
3. Once done, allow to release pressure naturally for 10 minutes then release remaining using quick release. Remove lid.
4. Blend pudding mixture using an immersion blender until smooth.
5. Serve and enjoy.

Nutrition Info:
- Calories 205 Fat 8.6 g Carbohydrates 29.1 g Sugar 9 g Protein 2.6 g Cholesterol 0 mg

Ricotta Ramekins

Servings: 4
Cooking Time: 1 Hour

Ingredients:
- 6 eggs, whisked
- 1 and ½ pounds ricotta cheese, soft
- ½ pound stevia
- 1 teaspoon vanilla extract
- ½ teaspoon baking powder
- Cooking spray

Directions:
1. In a bowl, mix the eggs with the ricotta and the other ingredients except the cooking spray and whisk well.
2. Grease 4 ramekins with the cooking spray, pour the ricotta cream in each and bake at 360 degrees F for 1 hour.
3. Serve cold.

Nutrition Info:
- calories 180, fat 5.3, fiber 5.4, carbs 11.5, protein 4

RECIPES

DATE

RECIPES	Salads	Meats	Soups
SERVES	Grains	Seafood	Snack
PREP TIME	Breads	Vegetables	Breakfast
COOK TIME	Appetizers	Desserts	Lunch
FROM THE KITCHEN OF	Main Dishes	Beverages	Dinners

INGREDIENTS

DIRECTIONS

NOTES

SERVING ☆☆☆☆☆

DIFFICULTY ☆☆☆☆☆

OVERALL ☆☆☆☆☆

BASIC KITCHEN CONVERSIONS & EQUIVALENTS

DRY MEASUREMENTS CONVERSION CHART

3 TEASPOONS = 1 TABLESPOON = 1/16 CUP

6 TEASPOONS = 2 TABLESPOONS = 1/8 CUP

12 TEASPOONS = 4 TABLESPOONS = 1/4 CUP

24 TEASPOONS = 8 TABLESPOONS = 1/2 CUP

36 TEASPOONS = 12 TABLESPOONS = 3/4 CUP

48 TEASPOONS = 16 TABLESPOONS = 1 CUP

METRIC TO US COOKING CONVERSIONS

OVEN TEMPERATURES

120 °C = 250 °F

160 °C = 320 °F

180° C = 350 °F

205 °C = 400 °F

220 °C = 425 °F

LIQUID MEASUREMENTS CONVERSION CHART

8 FLUID OUNCES = 1 CUP = 1/2 PINT = 1/4 QUART

16 FLUID OUNCES = 2 CUPS = 1 PINT = 1/2 QUART

32 FLUID OUNCES = 4 CUPS = 2 PINTS = 1 QUART

 = 1/4 GALLON

128 FLUID OUNCES = 16 CUPS = 8 PINTS = 4 QUARTS = 1 GALLON

BAKING IN GRAMS

1 CUP FLOUR = 140 GRAMS

1 CUP SUGAR = 150 GRAMS

1 CUP POWDERED SUGAR = 160 GRAMS

1 CUP HEAVY CREAM = 235 GRAMS

VOLUME

1 MILLILITER = 1/5 TEASPOON

5 ML = 1 TEASPOON

15 ML = 1 TABLESPOON

240 ML = 1 CUP OR 8 FLUID OUNCES

1 LITER = 34 FL. OUNCES

WEIGHT

1 GRAM = .035 OUNCES

100 GRAMS = 3.5 OUNCES

500 GRAMS = 1.1 POUNDS

1 KILOGRAM = 35 OUNCES

US TO METRIC COOKING CONVERSIONS

1/5 TSP = 1 ML

1 TSP = 5 ML

1 TBSP = 15 ML

1 FL OUNCE = 30 ML

1 CUP = 237 ML

1 PINT (2 CUPS) = 473 ML

1 QUART (4 CUPS) = .95 LITER

1 GALLON (16 CUPS) = 3.8 LITERS

1 OZ = 28 GRAMS

1 POUND = 454 GRAMS

BUTTER

1 CUP BUTTER = 2 STICKS = 8 OUNCES = 230 GRAMS = 8 TABLESPOONS

WHAT DOES 1 CUP EQUAL

1 CUP = 8 FLUID OUNCES

1 CUP = 16 TABLESPOONS

1 CUP = 48 TEASPOONS

1 CUP = 1/2 PINT

1 CUP = 1/4 QUART

1 CUP = 1/16 GALLON

1 CUP = 240 ML

BAKING PAN CONVERSIONS

1 CUP ALL-PURPOSE FLOUR = 4.5 OZ

1 CUP ROLLED OATS = 3 OZ 1 LARGE EGG = 1.7 OZ

1 CUP BUTTER = 8 OZ 1 CUP MILK = 8 OZ

1 CUP HEAVY CREAM = 8.4 OZ

1 CUP GRANULATED SUGAR = 7.1 OZ

1 CUP PACKED BROWN SUGAR = 7.75 OZ

1 CUP VEGETABLE OIL = 7.7 OZ

1 CUP UNSIFTED POWDERED SUGAR = 4.4 OZ

BAKING PAN CONVERSIONS

9-INCH ROUND CAKE PAN = 12 CUPS

10-INCH TUBE PAN =16 CUPS

11-INCH BUNDT PAN = 12 CUPS

9-INCH SPRINGFORM PAN = 10 CUPS

9 X 5 INCH LOAF PAN = 8 CUPS

9-INCH SQUARE PAN = 8 CUPS

Shopping List

A

Artichoke
Creamy Artichoke Dip 27
Sage Artichokes 31
Instant Pot Artichoke Hearts 33

Asparagus
Orange, Dates And Asparagus On Quinoa Salad 66
Dill, Havarti & Asparagus Frittata 87

Avocado
Avocado Toast 16
Avocado Dip 25
Avocado Salad 34

B

Bacon
Bacon, Spinach And Tomato Sandwich 17
Bacon, Vegetable And Parmesan Combo 18
Bacon And Tomato Pasta 74
Bacon & Hot Dogs Omelet 87

Banana
Banana Quinoa 19
Paleo Almond Banana Pancakes 89
St. Valentine's Mediterranean Pancakes 90
Cold Lemon Squares 95

Bean
Beans And Spinach Mediterranean Salad 63
Kidney Beans And Beet Salad 66

Beef
Garlic Scrambled Eggs 18
Greek Beef Meatballs 43
Flavors Taco Rice Bowl 65
Beef-stuffed Baked Potatoes 76
Tomato And Beef Casserole 77
Square Meat Pies (sfeeha) 80
Beef Meatballs 80
Bean Beef Chili 81
La Paz Batchoy (beef Noodle Soup La Paz Style) 81

Beef Sirloin
Kefta Styled Beef Patties With Cucumber Salad 63
Beef And Grape Sauce 77
Beef And Celery Stew 81

Beef Steak
Spice-rubbed Beef Steaks 40
Pepper Steak Taco 79

Beet
Beet Spread 27

Berry
Fruity Salad 70

Black Bean
Black Beans And Quinoa 64

Black Olives
Cheesy Olives Bread 20

Blackberry
Blackberry Jam 95

Blue Cheese
Blue Cheese And Arugula Salad 74

Bread
Mediterranean Grilled Cheese Sandwiches 31

Broccoli
Tortellini Salad With Broccoli 60

C

Cabbage
Fresh And Light Cabbage Salad 70
Tuscan Cabbage Soup 89

Calamari
Dill Calamari 57
Calamari Mediterranean 24

Carrot
Hoemade Egg Drop Soup 29
Cardamom And Carrot Soup 30
Lemony Carrots 73
Veal Shank Barley Soup 87